100
Festive Finds in Missouri
Festivals, Fairs, and Other Fun Events

ANN HAZELWOOD

REEDY PRESS

St. Louis, Missouri

Reedy Press
PO Box 5131
St. Louis, MO 63139, USA

Library of Congress Control Number: 2010924853

ISBN: 978-1-933370-59-0

Please visit our website at www.reedypress.com.

Printed in the United States of America
10 11 12 13 14   5 4 3 2 1

CONTENTS

DEDICATION

Growing up in a small community, I remember looking forward to any event that would interrupt our routine and brighten the day. Such diversions provided many fond memories that found their way into our conversations for quite some time.

Having been an event organizer myself, I have a great deal of respect for the community leaders who volunteer their time to make the events and festivals in this book possible. Their hard work gives so much joy to so many, and I salute them.

I'd also like to dedicate this book to all the Missouri chamber directors, park directors, tourism directors, economic development directors, and their staff members who routinely go above and beyond the call of duty to remind that what it is in their job descriptions is only part of their job. You all are a credit to your organizations.

And to those who are beginning to create more "festive finds" for us to enjoy, I encourage you in your efforts. The rewards are great—and greatly appreciated!

FOREWORD

There are more than seven hundred towns in Missouri, and I've seen them all. Over the course of a year, by my count, these towns stage nearly 2.3 billion festivals and events. All of them are good. But if your time is valuable, use this book as your guide.

It reminds me of the game we played in our younger years: "If you were stuck on a desert island and could only take 100 albums. . . ." Ann Hazelwood has picked some of my favorites, and even a few I've put on my list to attend.

Start planning your list, too. I'll see you on the road.

—John Robinson, former Missouri tourism director, has driven every mile of every road on Missouri's highway map. He documents his travels in his King of the Road *column in* Missouri Life Magazine

INTRODUCTION

Nearly every week, there is a festival or event in Missouri. When I learn of a significant attraction—something unique and truly inventive—it piques my curiosity and inspires me to explore it further.

I usually can find something clever or fun at most festivals and events. Ask a variety of people, though, and you will get a variety of answers to what they liked most about it, and the things they tend to remember. Perhaps it's an unusual food or drink. Maybe it's a never-before-experienced activity. In researching this guide, I sought out those special touches, those unique finds that would make you want to pack the book, jump in the car, and check it out.

Missouri is a festive state, and Missourians are festival-seeking people. We like to celebrate our role in U.S. history with events like Lewis and Clark Heritage Days in St. Charles. We flock to food-themed celebrations like the Mushroom Festival in Richmond. We're game for Kansas City's Scottish Highland Games.

Creating the best, most memorable festivals, of course, is hard work that involves meticulous planning and extensive, behind-the-scenes effort. No sooner does one year's event end than preparations for next year begin. The best, most dedicated organizers sweat the details, ensuring that their food and activities match the theme of the event. And in many cases, events compete for the same weekends throughout the state, so they strive to outdo one another and look for ways to improve their event from the year before. The best of those attempt to entertain and educate us at the same time.

The winner in all of this is you, which is why I chose the best among Missouri's countless "festive finds" to share in this edition. I hope you enjoy them as much as I did.

100
Festive Finds in Missouri

1. COLUMBIA HEADS TO THE BOX OFFICE

Columbia is perhaps best known as the home of the University of Missouri, where education has been a central part of the community since its establishment in 1821. Columbia frequently rates among the best places to live, raise a family, and retire, ranking second nationally on *Money Magazine's* 1999 list of the Best Small Cities in America.

Turns out there's yet another reason to visit Columbia: the movies. Sundance, Toronto, and Cannes showcase the top directors, producers, and stars from the television and film industries, but Columbia has carved out its own niche in entertainment circles with the TRUE/FALSE FILM FEST. The festival, specializing in documentaries, has been offering fresh reviews of original, non-fiction films since 2003.

Co-founders Paul Sturtz and David Wilson say they named their event the True/False Film Fest in keeping with its open-minded, open-ended approach. You, the viewer, can decide what is true and false from among the roughly thirty-five full-length documentaries and two dozen or so short films screened each year, creating no shortage of thought-provoking conversation.

Downtown Columbia has embraced the festival, which spreads out to include such venues as the Blue Note, Ragtime Cinema, the Missouri Theater Center for the Arts, the Tiger Ballroom at the Forest Theater, Stephens College, Macklanburg Playhouse, Windsor Auditorium, and the Den. All are within walking distance of each other.

The festival's educational component is probably the best find of all, including the SWAMI program, which provides aspiring filmmakers with the opportunity to work with and learn from professionals.

Tickets can be scarce for the most popular events, so you might want to consider purchasing the festival's all-events pass. Also, note the ticket codes. "NRT" indicates that no reserved tickets remain. "Q" tickets require that you arrive thirty minutes early and stand in line in hopes of getting in five minutes before the show. "Q" ticket holders receive priority.

The festival's unique, "anything goes" March to March parade kicks off the event, held annually during the last week in February.

WHEN: Last week in February
WHERE: Theaters in Columbia
NEARBY ATTRACTION: University of Missouri Cultural Heritage Center
INFO: 573-442-TRUE; http://www.truefalse.org; www.visitcolumbiamo.com

2. CHRISTMAS AROUND THE WORLD

Smack in the middle of America's heartland is an event that recognizes Christmas on an international scale. The ST. CHARLES CHRISTMAS TRADITIONS FESTIVAL is a month-long celebration centered on historic Main Street, where white lights and greens encircle the lamp posts, handmade bows adorn buildings, and enchanting 1800s architecture serves as the backdrop for an international parade of Santas along fourteen blocks of specialty shops, museums, homes, and restaurants.

Visitors of every age and nearly every background will find their favorite gift-giver depicted at the Christmas Traditions Festival. From Germany comes Kris Kringle, along with Clara and her magical Nutcracker. Santa Lucia and Jack Frost represent Scandinavia's Norway, Sweden, and Denmark. Italy's La Befana, who delivers gifts to children on Epiphany Eve, cheers onlookers with her sense of humor and colorful dress. From Denmark comes the beautiful Snow Queen, and representing England are the Flower Girl,

WHEN: Day after Thanksgiving through Christmas Eve
WHERE: Historic Main Street, St. Charles
NEARBY ATTRACTION: Jehling Hardware's Holiday Train Display
INFO: 1-800-366-2427; www.stcharleschristmas.com; www.historicstcharles.com

Father Christmas, the Town Crier, and Charles Dickens's timeless novella *A Christmas Carol*, featuring favorite characters like Tiny Tim, Bob Cratchit, and Ebenezer Scrooge.

Representing America are Civil War Santa, Mrs. Claus, Frontier Santa, and Mother Goose. Russia's St. Nicholas makes an appearance, as does France's Pere Noel, who fills children's shoes with gifts on Christmas Eve. Of course, no Christmas Traditions Festival would be complete without the North Pole and its elves and reindeer. Rounding out the atmosphere, carolers stroll through the streets and the Christmas Angel and Sugar Plum Fairy flutter about, both outfitted in dazzling, authentic, colorful costumes.

Each character, including the many versions of Santa, offers a complimentary, collectible photo card. Follow the entertainers along the parade route to collect as many photos as possible. Other highlights include tasty chestnuts roasted over an open fire and children's visits with Santa.

3. Look, Live, and Learn

Perhaps you have visited the Daniel Boone Home in Defiance. But have you truly experienced it?

Take advantage of the opportunity to live like an early 1800s frontiersman or woman at Boone's homestead in the Femme Osage Valley during the annual, two-day PIONEER DAYS celebration.

Re-enactors in authentic era costumes at Boonesfield Village teach skills like open-hearth cooking, metal working, blacksmithing, and colonial gardening. Transport yourself some two hundred years back in time to a historic village featuring a dozen buildings spread across rolling grounds and including a charming wedding chapel, general store, the Mt. Hope Schoolhouse, and a millinery shop specializing in women's hats.

The best find in the village is Daniel Boone's original home, where he lived until his death in 1820. The two hundred-year-old structure, built with limestone walls two feet thick, boasts four floors, seven fireplaces, and a ballroom on the third floor. It is now a national historic site.

Lindenwood University, located in St. Charles, owns the grounds where reconstruction of the Boone family's farm is taking place. Special events like the annual Candlelight Tour draw huge crowds each Christmas season.

WHEN: Two weekends in December
WHERE: 1868 Hwy. F, Defiance
NEARBY ATTRACTIONS: Numerous wineries in this "wine country"
INFO: 636-798-2005; www.lindenwood.edu/boone

4. ALL THAT JAZZ!

The COLEMAN HAWKINS LEGACY JAZZ FESTIVAL in St. Joseph celebrates a true jazz pioneer. Coleman Hawkins, born on November 21, 1904, in St. Joseph, traveled the country learning from and playing with the best musicians, including Louis Armstrong. Hawkins's signature instrument was the tenor saxophone, and he was the first jazz musician to use it as a lead instrument in his bands.

Hawkins performed with some of jazz's legendary groups, including Mamie Smith's Jazz Hounds and Fletcher Henderson's Orchestra, with whom he played until 1934, when he struck out on his own and eventually became "Father of the Tenor Sax." Hawkins's profile and fame expanded in the 1950s, when he appeared on the *Tonight Show*, and he continued to play until his last concert in Chicago in 1969. He died in New York in May 1969.

In 1998, the St. Joseph Coleman Hawkins Jazz Society was formed, and in 2003 the city approved adding the name Coleman Hawkins Park to its existing Felix Street Square. The park has an eight-foot statue of Hawkins, which was constructed in 2008.

To celebrate the jazz he loved so much, the Coleman Hawkins Jazz Festival features a sampling of sounds ranging from big band music of the 1940s and 1950s to the best in contemporary and Latin jazz. The 1939 recording of "Body and Soul," the pop standard that brought Hawkins international recognition, is among the festival's mainstays and most popular performances.

On a side note, St. Joseph became a destination point for the Hannibal–St. Joseph Railroad Company, which went hand-in-hand with the city's becoming the site of the Pony Express Headquarters in 1860. Each continue to give St. Joseph growth and prosperity, although it was Hawkins who gave St. Joseph the right to stake its claim as the birthplace of one of jazz's true innovators.

WHEN: Second weekend in June
WHERE: Seventh and Felix streets, St. Joseph
NEARBY ATTRACTION: Pony Express Museum
INFO: 800-785-0360; www.stjomo.com; www.colemanhawkins.org

5. A German Immigrant's Dream

When some seven hundred German immigrants arrived in Frohna in 1839, little did they realize the area's beautiful, lush hills and valleys would become a tourism destination.

The SAXON LUTHERAN MEMORIAL FALL FESTIVAL takes place each year on the second Saturday in October on property originally owned by Thomas Twyman, who moved to Frohna from North Carolina and began building a log cabin village. Brothers Wilhelm and Christian Bergt purchased Twyman's plot, and members of the Bergt family lived there continuously until 1957. The settlement is listed on the National Register of Historic Places.

The restored village of log cabins, a barn, a blacksmith shop, and a schoolhouse provides a step back to a slower, simpler time, and the festival's highlight is the outdoor baking oven, where traditional bakers turn out fresh bread and other foods. The festival features numerous, fascinating food-preparation demonstrations, all with a German flair, including the production of buttermilk, homemade apple butter, molasses, and cooked cheese. Generations of visitors have enjoyed the region's unforgettable coffee cake. Fresh blackberry, cherry, and peanut butter are among other festival favorites, as well as pork burgers, barbeque, and sausages.

Entertainment is centered around a portable-wagon stage decorated with fall leaves and pumpkins. There, singing groups perform, tantalizing the crowd with a memorable rendition of the traditional sing-along Schnitzelbaum song. The festival also includes craft demonstrations and re-enactments of the hard work that took place in the mid-1800s such as log splitting and livestock butchering.

Frohna has only 192 year-round residents, many of whom work at the East Perry Lumber Company, owned by Frohna natives who have put their town on the map with their extensive logging and sawmilling operation. The mill was founded in 1945, and a third generation of owners continues to operate it successfully.

WHEN: Second Saturday in October
WHERE: 296 Saxon Memorial Drive, Frohna
NEARBY ATTRACTION: Lutheran Heritage Museum
INFO: 573-824-5404; www.saxonlutheranmemorial.com

6. POPULAR PUMPKIN PARTY

Hartsburg is home to 108 residents, thousands of pumpkins, and one unique event—the annual PUMPKIN FEST—that makes this tiny town a heavy hitter in Missouri tourism circles. Approximately fifty-five thousand visitors each year attend the two-day Pumpkin Fest, a community-produced event that has earned the Little Mouse That Roared award from the Missouri Division of Tourism and that organizers manage to produce for under twenty thousand dollars.

The Pumpkin Fest parade is a highlight of an event that also includes pumpkin crafts and a pie-eating contest. One unexpected, if pleasant find is the challenging Corn Maze.

Originating in 1991, the festival has been held every year but 1993, when Missouri experienced heavy flooding that severely damaged pumpkin crops. The event falls right in the middle of harvest season, bringing thousands of visitors to Hartsburg at a time when gorgeous, seasonal fall foliage lines the town's Katy Trail and the nearby Missouri River. Among other Hartsburg attractions are a woodcarver, bed and breakfast, winery, art gallery, cafe, and a produce farm.

WHEN: Second weekend in October
WHERE: Along the Katy Trail off 179, Hartsburg
NEARBY ATTRACTION: Jefferson City, the state capitol
INFO: www.hartsburgpumpkinfest.com

7. What's Hot in Missouri?

In Missouri, as elsewhere, chili isn't just a winter dish. No matter what time of the year, Missourians love and appreciate good chili. In that vein, the International Chili Society claims it is the "home of the chili heads," and the society's exposure and guidance ensures events like the MISSOURI STATE CHILI COOK-OFF in Maryland Heights remain successful year in and year out.

This is no free-for-all chili-making contest. There are rules to follow and specific categories in every contest. You might be surprised to find that the Traditional Red Chile category encompasses any kind of red meat or combination of meats cooked with red chili peppers and various spices. Beans and pasta are strictly forbidden. Chile Verde is similar, except it's made with green chili peppers.

The rules also state that no ingredient can be pre-cooked, except canned or bottled tomatoes or sauces. One of the more fascinating aspects of the cook-offs is the judging. The key characteristics of judging good chili are taste, consistency, aroma, color, and bite. And be warned, the bite can be significant!

The cook-off also includes a salsa competition without rules. Unlike the chili, salsa doesn't have to be made on site.

Like other cook-offs around the state, the Maryland Heights event includes other attractions like music, crafts, and games, as well as unique chili varieties such as white chili and vegetarian chili. Chili cook-offs elsewhere in Missouri include two Home Grown Folk Festival District Cook-Offs in Troy, the Clarksville Regional Cook-Off, and the Lupus Chili Cook-Off. Awards and cash prizes vary by location.

What a great way to find out what's "hot" in Missouri!

WHEN: Last Saturday in September
WHERE: Westport Plaza, Maryland Heights
NEARBY ATTRACTION: Westport Shopping Center
INFO: www.chilicookoff.com

8. A Blooming Good Time

Charleston began to bloom in 1837, when an original settler of Mississippi County sold twenty-two acres to Joseph Moore for $337. Now the city shares its beautiful dogwoods and azaleas with visitors from around Missouri and beyond at its annual spring DOGWOOD-AZALEA FESTIVAL, held the third weekend in April.

The flowering trees and shrubs will attract you to the festival, but a variety of other events will keep you there. Activities include a quilt show, plant sale, house and garden tours, 5K race, piano concert, swine races, exotic animal petting zoo, train show, fish fry, ice cream social, queen contest, carnival, arts and crafts show, fine art show, and one of the largest festival parades in the area.

The real find at the festival, though, is the visual and aromatic treat of enjoying the colors and fragrances of the six-mile tour of blossoming flowers. Tours can be arranged via a free shuttle, with romantic carriage rides also available.

If that's not enough, the festival sports a unique nighttime feature, in which residents turn some six thousand spotlights on the banks of azaleas and white lights twinkle on the trees during the twilight tour. For a real treat, try walking the nighttime route.

A second evening event, the Bloomin' Candlelight Review Show at the Clara Drinkwater Newman Auditorium, showcases talented musicians providing free entertainment.

You're virtually assured of a "blooming" good time.

> **WHEN:** Third weekend in April
> **WHERE:** Downtown Main Street, Charleston
> **NEARBY ATTRACTION:** The home of former Missouri Governor Warren E. Hearnes
> **INFO:** 573-683-6509; www.charlestonmo.org

9. CELEBRATING WALT DISNEY

Walt Disney's boyhood home of Marceline is where the famous illustrator first dreamed up so many of his characters, and it's also the site of an annual event in his honor, the TOONFEST. The Disney connection attracts nationally known cartoonists to the town to display their work, host seminars, and demonstrate their drawing skills.

The event begins with a unique, unforgettable parade starring the guest artists and complete with Disney-themed floats that will transport you back to your childhood with memories of Donald Duck, Mickey and Minnie Mouse, and other Disney favorites. Other highlights of Toonfest include a series of cartoon symposiums at Uptown Theater and cartoon shows at the Masonic Temple. Cartoons aren't always for kids, of course, but Toonfest's best find has a youthful slant. Student Day is a free educational day for high school, college, and home-schooled students, who are invited to enroll in cartooning, graphic design, animation, or journalism sessions. Lunch and transportation are free.

For the even younger set, tea parties and the Yellow Creek Pirates are featured attractions, while makeup artists are on hand to create princesses in a fun event called Bangels, Baubles and Beads.

Not surprisingly, the Disney name is ubiquitous in Marceline. Walt's barn is where he and his sister frequently played. There, a cottonwood tree—known as the Dreaming Tree—still stands, marking the creative haven that inspired Disney's ideas. A park, pool, and even the U.S. Post Office bear his name.

Tours are available through Disney's childhood home, now called the Hometown Museum. Disney claimed more things of importance happened to him in Marceline than anywhere else. The Toonfest is an opportunity to see firsthand why that's true.

WHEN: Third Saturday in September
WHERE: Main Street and Ripley Park, Marceline
NEARBY ATTRACTION: World War I General John J. Pershing's home in Laclede
INFO: 660-376-9258; www.toonfest.net

10. Let Us Break Bread

The chamber of commerce in Chillicothe isn't shy about touting this charming town's claim to fame—the discovery of the first automatic bread-slicing machine, which made its debut in 1928 and revolutionized the baking industry. The city cleverly capitalized on its nugget of historic trivia, proclaiming Chillicothe as "the best thing since sliced bread," a slogan featured on its promotional material and prominently painted on a mural across a downtown building. In fact, the most visually alluring finds in Chillicothe are the many murals on every street corner, spurring newly arrived visitors to pull over and view the impressive life-size paintings up close.

Among the centerpieces of the city's Chautauqua in the Park Festival is the aptly named BREADFEST, attracting top bakers from all around to compete for cash prizes, with $250 going to the winner in each category. Varieties include best bread, best yeast bread, most sliceable, and a best bread youth category. Participants pay a one dollar per loaf entry fee, and mailed entries are acceptable. A panel of judges rates each entry on taste, texture, appearance, and sliceability.

Whatever your reason, I can't think of a better place to break bread than Chillicothe.

WHEN: First weekend in September
WHERE: Rotary Shelter House at Simpson Park, Chillicothe
NEARBY ATTRACTION: Grand River Area Family YMCA
INFO: 660-646-4050; www.homeofslicedbread.com

11. How Sweet It Is

Each year, the tiny town of East Prairie takes a break from the long, hot summer to celebrate the local harvest with its SWEETCORN FESTIVAL, which has been in existence for thirty-five years. Sponsored by the East Prairie Chamber of Commerce, the unique festival is a treat for corn lovers, cyclists, and bargain hunters alike. Where else can you find a corn-shucking contest, or attend a Corn Pickin' Flea Market?

The biggest find at the festival is the Tour de Corn, in which hundreds of cyclists compete in events of fifteen, thirty-six, and one hundred miles. Local cyclist Mike Bryant believed an event like this could raise money for charity in a big way, and it's a ride unlike any other you will find across the country. Rest stops for the cyclists offer sweet corn and homemade cookies along the scenic, rural highway.

The party starts on Main Street on Friday and builds to July 4, when the festival culminates with fireworks and a parade. Other highlights include a fish fry, street dance, and car show.

East Prairie is home to more than three thousand people and is located at the top of Missouri's boot heel. Founded in 1883 by the St. Louis Southwestern Railway Company, its history and its residents' dedication to improving their quality of life has earned it Missouri Community Betterment awards. In 1994, East Prairie was named an "enterprise community," a distinction not usually given to such a small rural town.

The Sweetcorn Festival is a glowing example of that enterprising spirit.

WHEN: Last weekend in June through July 4
WHERE: 219 N. Washington Street, East Prairie
NEARBY ATTRACTION: Big Oak Tree State Park
INFO: 573-649-3057; www.eastprairiemo.net

12. World's Top Holiday Event

The notion that Branson is the preferred place to celebrate Christmas isn't confined to the Midwest. CNN.com says CHRISTMAS IN BRANSON is the best find of the holiday season.

Interestingly, Branson is relatively new to such holiday bustle. Until twenty years ago, November and December were fairly quiet months in this tourist town, which has since exploded in popularity as the Live Music Capital of the World and earned the honor of being one of the top Christmas destinations in the country.

The best find at this glorious event is the five-story Christmas tree, complete with special effects, on display in the middle of Main Street. Some 300,000 lights cover the tree, flashing in sync to music, and another 450,000 lights adorn the surrounding ten store fronts and 250 cut pine trees.

An estimated 350,000 visitors attend the spectacle each year, and many of them also take in one of the many Christmas shows featuring celebrities like Andy Williams, who croons whimsically about the "most wonderful time of the year." The full lineup of shows appeals to various age groups and tastes, as evidenced by busloads and lines of cars continually passing through what has become a magical town that attracts 8.4 million visitors overall each year. The former riverboat stop now boasts forty theaters, seventy live shows, and two hundred lodging facilities. Three lakes, nine golf courses, two hundred retail outlets, numerous caves, and other year-round attractions make Branson a popular destination spot for visitors from around the world.

Branson no doubt has helped put Missouri on the Christmas entertainment map with its memorable, if relatively recent ascent as a holiday heavyweight.

WHEN: November 1 to New Year's Eve
WHERE: 165 Expressway Lane, downtown Branson
NEARBY ATTRACTION: The Titanic Museum
INFO: 800-800-2019; 800-214-3661; www.explorebranson.com

13. THE CITY OF WATERS

Since 1880, visitors have traveled to the valley of Excelsior Springs to experience the healing waters that flowed from what was then known as Siloam Spring. Word spread quickly of the water's ability to heal, and around owner A. W. Wyman's spring a community sprouted, dotting the landscape with homes, a dry goods store, and a church. Wyman named the town after Henry Wadsworth Longfellow's well-known poem. From twenty separate springs flow four distinct varieties of mineral water credited with healing properties that have helped enhance its reputation, and in 1927 a Hall of Waters was built for tourists to enjoy samples.

It's only fitting, then, that Excelsior Springs should celebrate its heritage with WATERFEST, a three-day event sponsored by its chamber of commerce. Activities include crafters, artists, dog racing, a children's carnival, balloon rides, games, bike and car shows, a beer garden, a farmer's market, a quilt show, live music, and a grand fireworks display on Saturday evening. The fest's biggest find is even bigger than the spring water—the Elms Hotel. This grand hotel sprang up to provide lodging for the many visitors who came to soak up the mineral waters and sun themselves in the beautiful surrounding gardens.

The Elms survived two fires, its lavish layout and exquisite ballroom drawing the attention of dignitaries and U.S. presidents, once serving as a getaway for presidential candidate Harry S. Truman during the hectic 1948 campaign. Truman and his Secret Service bodyguards slept in room 300, and the future president relaxed in the mineral baths and enjoyed salt rubs and a massage. He then retired to his room to listen to gloomy election results, going to bed convinced he had lost. He awoke the next morning only to discover he did in fact win the election—despite the now-infamous "Dewey Defeats Truman" headlines—and left quickly for the Democratic headquarters in Kansas City. The next day, however, he returned to the Elms Hotel and addressed the public in a celebratory news conference that further raised the profile of this mineral spring resort.

Oozing history—if only its walls could talk—the Elms Hotel continues to be a popular destination today and is an integral part of the activities during the Waterfest event.

> **WHEN:** Last weekend in June
> **WHERE:** 401 Regents Street, Excelsior Springs
> **NEARBY ATTRACTION:** Watkins Mill State Park
> **INFO:** 816-630-0750; www.cityofesmo.com;
> www.elmsresort.com

14. FOLK MUSIC AT ITS BEST

One of Missouri's best-known music events is the BIG MUDDY FOLK FESTIVAL in Boonville, hosted for nearly twenty years at historic Thespian Hall. Created in 1838 when sixty Boonville men formed a dramatic club called the Thespian Society, the hall was built with ornate seating and gingerbread architecture, and adapted over the years to accommodate performers and audience members. Always under the threat of destruction, Thespian Hall received a reprieve when it was placed on the National Register of Historic Places as the oldest theater west of the Allegheny Mountains. Restoration is ongoing and now is in the hands of the Friends of Historic Boonville.

Well known as Thespian Hall is to Missourians, the folk festival put it—and Boonville—on the map. The hall sits high on the bluff overlooking the Missouri River, providing a dramatic stage for well-known performers of traditional music, dance, and art.

Educational opportunities abound at this two-day event, which features workshops on fiddling, songwriting, jam sessions, storytelling, and popular song-swap sessions. Demonstrations are sprinkled here and there, with delicious barbeque to ensure you don't have to go far for a meal. Attendees pay twenty dollars per day or thirty-five dollars for the weekend.

WHEN: First weekend in April
WHERE: Thespian Hall, Boonville
NEARBY ATTRACTION: Historic Frederic Hotel
INFO: 888-588-1477; www.bigmuddy.org; www.folkjam.org

15. Oink, Oink and Gobble, Gobble!

The OZARK HAM AND TURKEY FESTIVAL gives California, Missouri's two largest businesses the opportunity to strut—and waddle—their stuff. Burgers Smokehouse represents the ham at the festival, and Honeysuckle White, a division of Cargill, Inc., provides the turkey at an event organized by the California Chamber of Commerce.

In one day, 25,000 visitors descend on this town of fewer than 5,000 to partake in a tasty event that also includes an antique and classic car show, 5K run, antique tractor show, diaper derby, washboard tournament, craft booths, horse show, and flea market. Carriage and pony rides parade visitors around the festival amid nonstop music playing from two stages.

Food, however, is clearly top of mind, beginning with an early morning ham breakfast, followed by two favorites—delicious turkey legs and country ham sandwiches. Steak sandwiches and barbeque also are popular choices. The festival's biggest find is the world's largest submarine sandwich, which stretches for nearly a full city block. Cargill workers build the sandwich and stuff it with goodies, then offer it to festival attendees at no charge. Burgers Smokehouse sponsors shuttles for tours and offers substantial discounts on its products.

Nicknamed the Country Ham Capital of the World, California is the county seat and is named after California Wilson, a logger who offered gallons of whiskey in exchange for having the town bear his name. It was incorporated in 1848. Trivia buffs will be interested in the fact that the *California Democrat* newspaper, opened in 1938, is the oldest business in Moniteau County.

California's motto says it all: "It's small enough to know you and large enough to serve you!" Ham and turkey, that is.

WHEN: Third Saturday in September
WHERE: Main and Oak streets, downtown California
NEARBY ATTRACTION: Cultural Heritage Center
INFO: www.calmo.com

16. Pow Wow

The town of Salem celebrates its Native American heritage by hosting the annual UPPER CURRENT RIVER POW WOW in cooperation with the Western Cherokee tribe. The event brings together old friends and creates new ones, providing the opportunity for Native Americans to get acquainted while educating visitors about their traditions in dancing, singing, cooking, and craftsmanship. Supported by donations, the Pow Wow's proceeds benefit the Salem Cultural Center.

While theories abound as to the event's actual origin, there is no debating its popularity. Pow Wow singers, long-prominent members of the Native American culture, play an important role in the dance performances, which feature a variety of songs that explore religion, society, and war. Songs sung in their native tongue are reminders to the Native American people of their old customs, while entertaining and educational for visitors.

When observers picture Pow Wows they probably think of the noise and vigor of the dances without knowing exactly what they are really watching. The real find at the Upper Current River Pow Wow is that most of the performances are social dances whose origins can easily be explained by observers familiar with them. Just as fashion evolves in other cultures, so it is with the costumes of the Native Americans.

Pow Wows traditionally begin with a grand parade, and this one is no different. Spectators are asked to stand and pay their respects to flag bearers carrying banners, and veterans display the U.S., tribunal, and the prisoner of war flags. The eagle staffs represent various tribes that are present at the Pow Wow. Audience participation is an integral part of the performances, and the performers seem to love the attention. Visitors are encouraged to bring folding chairs or blankets. There is an admission fee to enter the grounds, but seniors and children are free.

WHEN: Memorial Day
WHERE: 10th and Hickory streets, Salem
NEARBY ATTRACTION: Montauk State Park
INFO: www.salemmo.com

17. MISSOURI'S MUSHROOMS

No one better celebrates the Missouri mushroom than the folks in Richmond, where the delicious, homegrown delicacy is the star attraction of the town's annual MUSHROOM FESTIVAL. Why does this town make such a fuss over its mushrooms? Because Richmond residents claim that since 1980 no place has been able to collect more mushrooms in the spring. For nearly thirty years, the festival boasts that it has sold more than 150 pounds of fresh morel mushrooms in one day.

The event offers numerous varieties and delicacies of mushrooms, and some of the presentations are downright amusing. The really cool find: A contest sponsored by the *Daily News* of Richmond offers a fifty-dollar prize for the largest mushroom. The record mushroom tipped the scale at a whopping eighteen pounds.

Mushrooms aren't only offered as food; they're materials in clever crafts like carved wooden mushroom shapes, mushroom-embroidered items, kitchen items painted with mushroom designs, and even mushroom-themed appliqué hand towels. Other highlights include Little Miss Mushroom and Mister Mushroom contests, plenty of music, and a parade that winds through town before winding up at the popular beer garden.

In the unlikely event you have your fill of mushrooms, barbeque abounds, and the state-sanctioned barbeque championship cook-off takes place here as well. Richmond claims to be the Mushroom Capital of the World, and far be it from the rest of us to argue.

WHEN: First weekend in May
WHERE: Downtown Richmond
NEARBY ATTRACTION: The Y-shaped Ray County Museum
INFO: 816-776-6916; www.richmondchamber.org

18. Celebrating Ragtime

Born in Texarkana, Texas, musician Scott Joplin achieved some of his greatest success—and met and married his wife—in Sedalia. While living in Missouri, Joplin released "Maple Leaf Rag," ragtime's first hit, which went on to sell 75,000 copies in six months in 1899. By the time of Joplin's death in 1917, he had become commonly known as the King of Ragtime and built a reputation as a gifted songwriter, composer, and performer.

Sedalia celebrates its strong connection to this musical pioneer with the SCOTT JOPLIN RAGTIME FESTIVAL, which reminds visitors of Joplin's performances at the city's Maple Leaf Club and Black 400 Club, where he often could be found when not touring nationally.

Sponsored by the Scott Joplin International Ragtime Foundation, the Ragtime Festival brings together entertainment and education with concerts by ragtime musicians, dance lessons, and symposiums. International artists are featured hourly at tents scattered throughout the festival grounds, which includes several free venues along with dinner shows and concerts, which require an admission fee.

The festival kicks off on Thursday with perhaps its best find—the Ragtime Ball. A period celebration that encourages attendees to dress in the style of the turn-of-the-century ragtime era, the ball is a stunning procession of women in beaded dresses and empire waist gowns escorted by men in derbies, top hats, and spats.

The Scott Joplin Ragtime Store offers souvenirs along with a diverse collection of music and other gifts. Sedalia, established in 1860, also is home to the Missouri State Fair.

WHEN: First Thursday in June, through the weekend
WHERE: East Third Street, Sedalia
NEARBY ATTRACTION: The Sedalia murals, located at the
   Sedalia Municipal Building
INFO: 660-826-2271 or 800-827-5295; ci.sedalia.mo.us; www.scottjoplin.org

19. Homegrown, Hometown Fun

The town of Norborne, home to about eight hundred people, bears the name of founder Norborne B. Coats and takes time out each summer to celebrate Coats's distinction as the world's most prolific soybean producer.

A Missouri pioneer and civil engineer, Coats put his eponymous town on the map as Soybean Capital of the World, a title Norborne's Lions Club began honoring in 1982 by sponsoring a SOYBEAN FESTIVAL that has continued to grow every year.

The three-day event begins with a parade led by the Soybean King—a farmer chosen for being one of the season's most successful soybean promoters. Meanwhile, sample the flavored soy nuts available from the FFA alumni, visit the Soybean Patch's beer garden and enjoy music, or stop by the Cook Shack for fried fish and pork chops.

Friday is Kids Day, featuring a variety of games for kids of all ages. The festival's best find is the Ha Ha Show—think "Hee Haw"—at the Soybean Theater, where costumed local residents convene for performances, gags, and talent displays that will send you home with a smile.

While August is a busy harvesting month for the local soybean farmers, they take a break to rehearse for the show, and the Norborne Interested Citizens provide scripts and set up the stage for the "Hayseeds." Admission is three dollars for adults and one dollar for children.

WHEN: Second weekend in August
WHERE: Downtown Norborne
NEARBY ATTRACTION: The Hammer Museum
INFO: 660-542-0922; 660-593-3514

20. The Celebration of Words

For those with an appreciation for the artistic qualities of the written word, writer and reader come together in Springfield every other October to celebrate the MISSOURI LITERARY FESTIVAL.

The event boasts a lineup of guest speakers who address a variety of topics and also includes panel discussions and networking opportunities to help aspiring writers gain exposure and improve their skills. The goal of most every writer is to be published, and the Literary Festival puts writers in touch with publishers seeking new faces and fresh topics.

The best find at the festival is the Mix and Mingle, a popular meet-and-greet between attendees and authors that provides plenty of question-and-answer opportunities. Art, music, and entertainment are combined with children's entertainment such as storytelling. The festival also stages a poetry competition that has, in the past, been a hit among "Cowboy Poets."

Opening ceremonies for this jam-packed weekend of literary appreciation include dignitaries and recognized celebrities from the fields of writing and the arts. The festival lineup boasts more than forty writers, including Missouri's poet laureate. The complete list is available on the Missouri Association of Community Arts Agencies website.

This is one of many events sponsored by the Missouri Association of Community Arts Agencies (MACAA), a network of more than seventy art agencies and some 1,350 Missouri artists. The MACAA was formed in 1979 to create programs and services to meet the community needs.

WHEN: First weekend in October (biennial)
WHERE: Hammons Field and the Creamery Arts Center, Springfield
NEARBY ATTRACTION: Missouri State University
INFO: www.missouriliteraryfestival.org; www.macaa.net

21. A Boyhood Celebration

Among the many reasons to visit Hannibal is this—it's Mark Twain's hometown. Perhaps Twain's most famous character is Tom Sawyer, and Hannibal celebrates Sawyer—and Twain—at its annual TOM SAWYER DAYS on Fourth of July weekend.

In Twain's books, Tom Sawyer grew up in a Hannibal-inspired rivertown and turned the Mississippi River into his playground. Tom Sawyer Days, created in the 1950s, aims to recreate the most enchanting, memorable aspects of life on the mighty river.

Events include a parade of bands and floats, a Tom Sawyer and Becky Thatcher contest, frog-jumping contests, and arts and crafts displays. In a nod to Twain's classic book, perhaps the most charming find at Tom Sawyer Days is the National Fence Painting contest. According to the story, Tom was asked to paint Aunt Polly's fence, but schemed to get his friends to do it for him. The opening day of the contest, sponsored by the Hannibal Jaycees, is open to local boys ages ten to thirteen. The winner competes the next day in the state contest, with the overall winner receiving a trophy that goes to the office of the governor of the winner's home state. The winner also receives a five hundred dollar savings bond and plaque. There also is an over-thirty division. Unlike Tom Sawyer, contestants are expected to white-wash their own assigned section of fence, and they are judged on the authenticity of their costumes, speed, and accuracy of their painting.

The event also provides the opportunity to view Hannibal as Twain did, with visits to his restored home, his girlfriend Becky Thatcher's house, the riverboat, and the Mark Twain Cave. The Mark Twain Museum archives first-edition copies of Twain's books.

WHEN: July 2-4
WHERE: Downtown Hannibal
NEARBY ATTRACTION: Missouri's No. 1 Bed and Breakfast, Garth Mansion
INFO: 573-221-3231; www.hannibaljaycees.org; www.visithannibal.com

22. Irish Eyes Are Smiling

Kansas City's sizable Irish population honors and celebrates its roots at the annual IRISH FEST, a nonprofit, independent festival that attracts more than 90,000 attendees every Labor Day weekend to Crown Plaza. More than 1,500 volunteers coordinate what has become the fastest-growing Irish festival in the country. Its aim is to serve as gracious host to the local and regional community for a friendly, enjoyable weekend of Irish culture.

The festival accomplishes this with a blend of music and education, with contests lying at the heart of an event that attracts connoisseurs in the fields of stout brewing, knitting, photography, dancing, and baking.

Food choices are vast, but you can't go wrong with a traditional Irish dinner of fish and chips with a fried pickle on the side. Three large stages provide entertainment that encourages audience participation, and you just might find yourself dancing a jig in the street while watching the Okiuda Academy of Irish Dance performers.

Sunday Mass is held under a tent near the State Tree Stage at 9:30 a.m., and then the festival begins. Refreshments are served following the service.

Festival organizers have managed to keep the family oriented event affordable and fun, and it's twice been named Best Festival in KC in the Kansas City Convention and Visitors Association Visitors Choice Competition.

> **WHEN:** Labor Day weekend
> **WHERE:** Crown Plaza, Kansas City
> **NEARBY ATTRACTION:** Retail stores in the Plaza
> **INFO:** 816-997-0837; www.kcirishfest.com

23. The Expedition Celebration

More than two hundred years after Thomas Jefferson dispatched Meriwether Lewis and William Clark to explore lands acquired in the Louisiana Purchase, the Lewis and Clark expedition remains a source of fascination and a cause to celebrate. Lewis and Clark departed from St. Charles on May 16, 1804, with a crew of forty-three adventurous souls, and their exploits are recalled each year during LEWIS AND CLARK HERITAGE DAYS at Frontier Park.

St. Charles has celebrated Heritage Days since 1979, and the event includes a grand parade of colorfully uniformed fife and drum corps performers from around the country. Elsewhere in the park, re-enactors occupy military encampments, stage musket and cannon demonstrations, and play period music. Others, also in period character and dress, sell wares that include authentic clothing and crafts. The skillet-throwing contest offers a fun challenge and always draws crowds, and food is prepared in kettles and over open fires and served as it would have been in the early 1800s.

WHEN: Third weekend in May
WHERE: Frontier Park, St. Charles
NEARBY ATTRACTION: Lewis and Clark Boathouse and Nature Center
INFO: 800-366-2427; www.historicstcharles.com

The event's find is the collection of authentic keelboats and pirogues, all replicated in careful detail, that have launched from St. Charles for various expeditions. The boats are housed under the Lewis and Clark Museum at the river's edge.

24. Music All Around

For those who love blues and jazz music, Missouri offers some of the best the industry has to offer, and it doesn't sound any better than at the annual Kirksville ROUND BARN BLUES SHOW. Twice a year, blues fans can count on acoustically pleasing performances at this unique and unusual venue. And that's the real find—the circa 1913 round red barn is fully preserved and listed on the National Register of Historic Paces. The barn is the work of previous owner Benjamin Smith and current owner Dan Vogt, who added the Blues in the Round event and a restaurant.

The restaurant's Wooden Nickel section offers terrific barbeque and some of the best Missouri taters around. Also available are Round Barn souvenirs, including t-shirts, teddy bears, and other novelties.

The walls, floor, and beams are original, and the barn is sixty-four feet in diameter and sixty-one feet high, with a self-supporting ceiling. The round barn concept, which now is the only one of its kind left, was created not only to house livestock but also to store more than one hundred tons of loose hay. It includes seven wooden livestock stalls, fifty-four windows, and a thirty-six-rung ladder leading to a cupola.

Kirksville perhaps is most closely identified with Truman University, founded in 1876, which provides students with the unique opportunity to intern with a Missouri state legislator, public official, or state agency.

WHEN: May and September
WHERE: 2131 State Street P, Kirksville
NEARBY ATTRACTION: Thousand Hills State Park
INFO: 660-665-2760; www.roundbarnblues.com

25. Great to Be Greek

If you're Greek—or if you've ever wondered what it would be like to be Greek—check out the St. Louis GREEKFEST, held at the Assumption Greek Orthodox Church each May. The city's Greek community founded the church in 1940 in the heart of St. Louis, then renovated the building and added a school in 1948 to accommodate its growing parish at 1212 Academy. Ten years later, members purchased an existing Gothic church and moved the parish to the more convenient location. Finally, in 1978, the parish constructed a new basilica and community center on purchased land in Town and Country in St. Louis County.

The GreekFest celebrates the region's rich Greek heritage with live music and colorful folk dancers, games for the entire family, along with vendors offering wares from around the world, including clothing, art, religious icons, and spectacular jewelry. Not surprisingly, the food is the event's best find. For a unique taste experience you won't find at any other festival, try the lamb with Greek spices, or order a combo plate of goodies that includes Moussake (egg plant with beef and cheese), two Dolmathes (stuffed grapes), and spanakopita (spinach pie). Pastitsio is a tasty beef and pasta casserole that would go wonderfully with one of the Greek salads. And pastries like Baklava top off the meal.

WHEN: Third weekend in May
WHERE: Assumption Greek Orthodox Church, St. Louis
NEARBY ATTRACTION: West County Antique Mall
INFO: 314-966-2255; www.stlouisgreekfest.com

26. An "Apple of Your Eye" Parade

Nowadays we take parades for granted, but the APPLE BLOSSOM PARADE in St. Joseph began in an era when such events were rare and considered too lavish or too expensive for many communities.

Started in 1924, when cars were scarce, parade founder James Hunt plowed ahead and gathered interested parties at the Market Square. Kenmoor Orchid provided automobiles free of charge so parade participants could drive past the Connett Orchard to see the apple trees in bloom. The route began at the hotel, continued past the orchids near Wathena Methodist Church, and on to Troy and Blair, ending with a church supper.

Within two years an association was up and running to host the first Apple Blossom Festival. A crowd of 5,000 people attended and consumed 600 pounds of beef, 4,500 loaves of bread, untold quantities of ham, gallons of coffee, and countless apples prepared in a variety of dishes.

As the years progressed, the excitement and the event grew. Organizers added a beer garden, a Pony Express Antique Show, a Nitty Gritty Dirt Band concert, a street dance, a rodeo, and a demolition derby. By the 1950s, the event included a band contest beginning the morning of the parade and ending with massed bands playing the "Star Spangled Banner" just prior to starting the parade.

A series of organizations have taken charge of the event, which is now run almost entirely by the St. Joseph Downtown Association, the Convention and Visitors Bureau, the city of St. Joseph, and Buchanan County. The apple connection, of course, stems from St. Joseph's billing as the "Jonathan Apple District of the World."

WHEN: Third weekend in May
WHERE: Felix Street Square, St. Joseph
NEARBY ATTRACTION: Albrecht-Kemper Museum of Art
INFO: www.stjomo.com; www.appleblossomparade.com

27. THE SPIRIT OF THE FRENCH

Founded by French settlers in the early 1700s, Ste. Genevieve is the oldest town on the west bank of the Mississippi River and holds the distinction of having the largest concentration of French colonial buildings in the United States. Now a national landmark, Ste. Genevieve has a rich history as home to generations of miners, farmers, and fur traders and was a staging point for the Lewis and Clark expedition.

Residents of the town, which now relies mainly on tourism as its primary industry, celebrate the region's history with the annual FRENCH HERITAGE FESTIVAL, providing tours of many of some fifty homes built more than two hundred years ago and glimpses of French Colonial-style vertical log homes that once housed farmers and furriers. Ste. Genevieve's oldest home was built in 1784.

The festival marks some three hundred years of French culture, customs, and architecture and attracts hundreds of artisans and includes re-enactments in which actors don costumes to portray militia.

Clustered in the downtown area are exceptional folk music performances, wine tasting opportunities, and samples of great French cuisine. Performances include promenades and dances complete with guides to help visitors participate. Catch the "esprit" of the festival and you just might find yourself speaking a bit of French before the weekend is over.

WHEN: Second weekend in June
WHERE: Historic downtown Ste. Genevieve
NEARBY ATTRACTION: Hawn State Park
INFO: 800-373-7007; 314-883-7097; www.greatriverroad.com

28. GOT MILK?

As Missouri events go, DAIRY DAYS just might be one of the healthiest in our state, and it happens in Springfield on a working 270-acre dairy farm surrounded by subdivisions.

The Rutledge Wilson Community Farm Park had a coordinator that thought there should be something special planned to celebrate "National Dairy Day" in June, thus Dairy Days were born. The event provided opportunities for fun as well as education and aims to tell the story of life on a dairy farm.

Stations include milking demonstrations with different dairy cows and even offer an opportunity to try whole milk, 2 percent milk, and skim milk. For those who prefer to do more than watch, perhaps the event's best find is

> **WHEN:** Second weekend in June
> **WHERE:** 3825 West Farm Road 146, Springfield
> **NEARBY ATTRACTION:** The Battle of Wilson Creek
> **INFO:** 417-837-5949; 800-678-8767
>   www.parkboard.org
>   www.extendedstayspringfield.com

a large fiberglass Holstein cow where you can try your hand at milking. Another station gives visitors turns at churning butter and then tasting the result. Hayrides are available for all ages, and if you bring your dressed-up billy goat, there is a parade in which he can be judged for prizes.

A variety of refreshments, including dairy ice cream, is sold by the Parks Department, and after 5 p.m. there is good bluegrass music, topped off with a large bonfire.

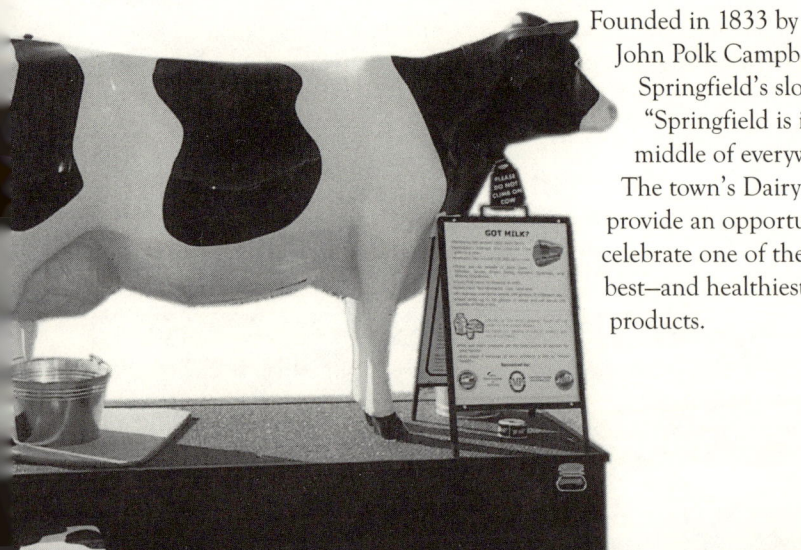

Founded in 1833 by John Polk Campbell, Springfield's slogan is "Springfield is in the middle of everywhere." The town's Dairy Days provide an opportunity to celebrate one of the state's best—and healthiest— products.

29. Candy for the Eyes and Mouth

Washington is one of those warm and charming Missouri towns you just never forget. Nestled into the hills along the Missouri riverfront, the town's charm is straight out of a storybook.

Most visitors identify Washington with the historic corncob pipe industry. Henry Tibbe and his son, Anton, began making corncob pipes in 1869 in its current location known as the Meerschaum Company. Aside from pipes, Washington stakes another claim as the heart of Missouri's wine country and host of the FINE ART FAIR AND WINEFEST each spring. The event takes place in a "wine pavilion" in Rennick Riverfront Park. More than sixty locally produced wines are poured at Missouri's largest wine-tasting event. Complimentary cheese and crackers are provided.

WHEN: Third weekend in May
WHERE: Rennick Riverfront Park and downtown Washington
NEARBY ATTRACTION: Meerschaum Pipe Factory
INFO: 636-239-1743; 888-7WASHMO; www.washmo.org

Participating wineries include: Adam Puchta Winery from Hermann; Augusta Winery from Augusta; Bias Vineyard and Winery/Gruhlke Microbrewery from Berge; Blumenhoff Vineyards from Dutzow; Montelle Winery from Augusta; Mt. Pleasant Winery from Augusta; Oak Glenn Winery from Hermann; Roblier Vineyard from New Haven; Stone Hill Winery from Hermann; La Dolce Vita Winery from Washington; and Sugar Creek Winery from Defiance. Should wine not satisfy your thirst, beer also is available.

One of the festival's great finds is an art fair held simultaneously with the tasting. Some fifty artists of all mediums display and sell their work and greet visitors throughout the weekend. The artists themselves are there for you to meet and chat. The outdoor location offers a free-flowing atmosphere, making it distinctive from festivals held in closed galleries. Live music each evening adds a romantic touch.

30. The Carpets of Chalk

Kansas City's popular Crown Center shopping and entertainment venue rests on massive squares of asphalt and concrete, and once a year this platform provides an amazing backdrop for colorful chalk artwork at the CHALK & WALK FESTIVAL.

The concept for this so-called "live" form of artwork evolves from street painting that was done in Italy centuries ago. Contemporary artists have brought the tradition to life with pastel chalks as the medium and pavement as their canvas.

The two-day event is always better with good weather, yet it is held rain or shine. Competitors of all ages can enter, and there is a separate area for children to draw at no charge with the help of an optional arts mentor.

For amateurs and professionals accustomed to working in the solace of their studio, the festival adds a unique element to the creative process, with crowds of on-lookers judging and making comments. Many of the large, colorful designs contain messages within the work. Some are serious interpretations of historic art, others simply wild and crazy original sketches. In both cases, the artists aim to expand your appreciation for their talents. The artists seem to love the companionship of other artists, and newcomers to the event say they are pleased at how seasoned chalk artists share their "tricks of the trade."

Other attractions include musicians and jugglers adding variety to the visual art that dominates the festival. This event is free and held each day from 11 a.m. to 8 p.m.

WHEN: Third weekend in June
WHERE: Crown Center Square, Kansas City
NEARBY ATTRACTION: Three levels of shopping at Crown Center
INFO: www.kcchalkandwalk.org

31. Around the World

You don't have to leave Missouri to enjoy entertainment and food from around the world. You can experience it all at the WORLD-FEST in Silver Dollar City at Branson.

In America's heartland, which is best known for American crafts, blue jeans, and cowboy boots, you can still enrich your taste for international culture through the variety of entertainment of laughter and music that is ubiquitous in this city within a city. At one stop, a band from Trinidad performs music from the Caribbean. At another, banjo music from New Zealand fills the air. Other performances include African drummers, dancers from Ghana, Russian acrobats, and Irish jiggers. Lest we forget, this culture traces its roots to the Ozarks region during the 1800s.

World-Fest wouldn't be complete without its best find, the delectable international cuisine available for sampling. Every country of the world is represented at the Tastes of the World exhibit at the park's Culinary and Craft School, where savory specialties and delicious desserts are made that weekend. How does Asian stir-fry sound with French crepes for dessert? The school is based in Branson year-round, but it enjoys the spotlight during World-Fest. Its three-thousand-square-foot, timber-frame building provides lovely views of the hollow from the back porch and showcases the latest in culinary technology and some of the top chefs in their field. Registration for classes is ten dollars per student.

Silver Dollar City is a destination unto itself and offers a variety of activities, including Kids Fest, the Southern Gospel Picnic, the Traditional Harvest Festival, an Ole Time Christmas Festival, and the Ole Bluegrass and Barbeque event.

WHEN: April-May
WHERE: Silver Dollar City, 399 Indian Point Road, Branson
NEARBY ATTRACTION: The Titanic Museum
INFO: www.reservebranson.com; www.silverdollarcity.com

32. Warm and Fuzzy

Is there a better combination than the arts and fun-loving animals? Not likely, which is why the two come together in Bethel for the ANNUAL WORLD SHEEP AND FIBER FESTIVAL, a packed weekend of activities such as sheep-calling and whistling contests, mutton busting, sheep shearing, and plenty of fun for the younger set, including the popular Piñata Bust.

The Lamb and Wool Queen is chosen not in the format of a traditional beauty contest, but rather for her knowledge of sheep as well as her involvement in the field, poise, and speaking ability. Yes, the title can go to a contestant of the opposite sex.

Many folks bring their sheep and goats to be shown or sold. All animals entering the grounds are subject to strict health requirements and are sold in the order of their arrival at the sale barn. A consignment is collected for each animal sold.

The festival's educational component comprises a long list of classes and workshops for beginners and the experienced alike, including knitting, weaving, over-dying, and needle-weaving.

The most intriguing find is the Sheep to Shawl competition, in which teams of three spinners and one weaver vie for the two hundred dollar top prize. Rules govern the varieties of fleece that can be used, and the loom must be pre-warped with a handspun warp of the contestant's choice. The warp can be dyed with a natural dye, or a commercial dye if a pattern is produced. Contestants need to produce their finished shawl with an eight-inch fringe. The winning shawl becomes the property of the festival and is displayed the following year. There is no entry fee.

WHEN: Saturday of Labor Day weekend
WHERE: Bethel Community Recreational area in Bethel
NEARBY ATTRACTION: Heartland Christian Academy
INFO: www.worldsheepfest.com

Along with the other events, vendors offer lovely handmade items perfect for snuggling, whether it's your newly purchased sheep or a new, hand-knit sweater.

33. Missouri's Little Italy

Celebrity chef Mario Batali of the Food Network calls the Hill in St. Louis "America's other Italy." COLUMBUS DAY is an ideal time to see for yourself! The Italian neighborhood in St. Louis celebrates Columbus Day as so many Italian-Americans do nationwide.

The city's Columbus Day Corporation claims to be the oldest Italian-American organization in the United States, incorporated in 1866 when many of St. Louis's Italian-American organizations joined forces to ensure there would always be a Columbus Day Parade and accompanying festivities.

This festival is held in Berra Park, a picturesque setting surrounded by tiny manicured houses and businesses that have flourished for generations. Bursts of red, green, and white decorate every float entry and vendor's booth and are the dominant hues on the hats of members of the Italian Community Band of St. Louis, who entertain audiences with traditional musical favorites. Unmistakable Italian warmth is in evidence everywhere, as hugs and kisses abound among the visitors who attend each year to renew acquaintances and seek out family and friends. Italians perhaps best express themselves with their love of food, and they love to share dishes such as spaghetti and meatballs, spiedini, and cannolis.

Honors of dedication and beauty also prevail during the Columbus Day activities. You'll find this loyalty and gratitude in many festivals and neighborhoods, but not quite like what you'll encounter on the Hill. The parade's grand marshal assumes a very prestigious position, and everyone recognizes his or her name and credentials. Awards are given out for the Spirit of Columbus and the Mother Cabrini.

Capping the event is the Miss Italian St. Louis Contest, where the winner stakes her claim to bragging rights for life.

WHEN: First Saturday in October
WHERE: Berra Park, St. Louis
NEARBY ATTRACTION: Bakeries and restaurants on every street corner
INFO: 314-647-6222; www.thehill-stl.org

34. IT'S ALL ABOUT APPLES

The Ozarks are alive and well in the lovely community of Versailles, where for more than thirty years the OLDE TYME APPLE FESTIVAL has drawn thousands of people together to enjoy the apples of the season.

The festival's reputation has earned it the title of Best Festival in Missouri for several years running, according to *Rural Missouri Magazine*.

Its greatness is judged on the caliber of its parade, where winners of the Baby Dumplin', Apple Dumplin', and Apple Darlin' contests are unveiled. Local bands, clowns, and themed floats add to the excitement, and a festival King and Queen contest is held at the Morgan County Courthouse.

A variety of music includes Dixieland jazz, country, gospel, and blues. The Royal Theater holds an annual Old Time Fiddler's contest that attracts the region's best fiddlers.

A surprise find is that the Apple Butter Days Fall Festival in Linn Creek is the following weekend and ties in nicely to this event. The apples are peeled, chopped, and transformed into apple butter in a large, traditional copper kettle, and then volunteers begin stirring and jarring. Selling it in quarts and pints, the apple butter is a hit and a big moneymaker. Fresh or frozen apple pies are available for take-home as well.

More than four hundred crafters set up at the Apple Festival and sell a variety of products and food related to the apple theme. There is nothing more American as apple pie, and the Midwest beauty of Versailles will make this town the apple of your eye!

WHEN: First weekend in October
WHERE: Downtown square, Versailles
NEARBY ATTRACTION: Morgan County Historical Museum
INFO: 573-378-4401; 800-386-5253; www.funlake.com; www.versailleschamber.com

35. A Very Cool Event

Visiting historic St. Charles is always a cool experience, but in the dead of winter nothing is cooler than the FETE DE GLACE.

Two blocks of the city's fourteen-block historic area are cordoned off for a massive ice-carving competition featuring two divisions—Master Carvers and Amateur. At 9:30 a.m. the master carvers are given five blocks of ice that must be carved by 12:00 a.m. More than one carver can work on a sculpture. The single-block carvers get one block of ice and must complete their sculptures by 3:30 p.m. Each block is forty-by-twenty-by-nine inches and weighs approximately 260 pounds.

Many of the carvers are chefs from all over the country, and they arrive with arsenals replete with tools like irons, chain saws, sanders, cold chisels, curling irons, and hand saws. Each carver has his own tent, and the sculptures are nothing short of amazing: Eagles, sports emblems, ships, nursery-rhyme characters, skiers, and celebrities are among the favorite subjects.

Weather conditions can vary, and inclimate conditions create an entirely new challenge. Rain is the ice carver's worst enemy and can cause the event to be cancelled. Sunshine can cause the ice to crack. Ideally, a cloudy or snowy day is perfect.

You might find that casting a vote for your favorite sculpture is the most fun of all. You get one vote in each division, and in the single-block and amateur category, there are first-, second-, and third-place awards given. There is only a first-place award given in the Master Carver division.

The Historic Downtown Association sponsors this free event, which features fire pits and endless cups of hot chocolate and coffee to keep visitors warm.

> **WHEN:** First Saturday in January
> **WHERE:** Historic North Main Street, St. Charles
> **NEARBY ATTRACTION:** Missouri's first state capitol building
> **INFO:** 636-724-0132; 800-366-2427; www.historicstcharles.com

36. Waynesville Goes Green

Waynesville turns green in the spring to celebrate its popular FROG FEST, a festival begun to honor and celebrate its famous frog, W. H. Croaker. This special frog is perched atop a cliff as you drive into Waynesville, and he traces his origins to a Department of Transportation rock-blasting project to widen the road, leaving a strange, frog-shaped structure peering over the highway.

The ladies at the Waynesville City Hall decided they'd ask a creative business person to fine-tune the shape and paint the frog in its natural colors. Encouraged by an enthusiastic response from residents, city leaders brainstormed to create an event that would have fun with the frog theme.

The event now includes two days of crafts, games, food, and entertainment centered in Waynesville's city park. Fun for all ages are the piñata and pony rides that take place daily. The ever-popular frog race is held in Roubidoux Creek and may include as many as eighty plastic, floatable frogs that race in two heats and are adopted by spectators. Savings bonds go to the winners.

Geared toward adults is the popular "Kiss a Frog" contest, in which three well-known individuals are chosen to represent a real frog. For a nominal fee, participants kiss the frog of their choice, then root for him or her to win. A Frog Queen is chosen each year and wears a traditional frog costume, and the festival also offers frog legs as a delicious dining option.

WHEN: First weekend in May
WHERE: City Park, Waynesville
NEARBY ATTRACTION: Roubidoux Creek Conservation Area; Route 66
INFO: 573-774-6171
www.waynesvillemo.org

37. Daring Donkeys and Mule Madness

Hold your horses! This unique event in Springfield is only about donkeys and mules, thus the OZARK MOUNTAIN MULE AND DONKEY DAYS festival. The Missouri mule always has been a signature part of our state, and it takes its rightful place, along with the donkey, at the Ozark Empire Fairgrounds in competitions that number more than sixty.

It starts on Friday with old-time music and an auction of select mules along with tack and equipment. Saturday night, the many skills of the mules and riders attract spectators to the arena, and among the fascinating finds is that the mules can race and even play football. Miniature donkeys participate in a costume contest, which leaves a lot to the imaginations of their owners. On Sunday, church services are held.

Many of the participants arrive at the event in an official festival wagon train that originates from twenty to twenty-five miles away. Before electing to participate in the wagon train be sure to check out the rules and information on taking part.

So what is a mule, you might ask? It's the offspring of a male donkey and a female horse. Horses and donkeys are a different species, and the size of a mule and his work purpose varies based on the breeding of the mule's dam. A mule makes a noise that starts with a whiney sound and ends with a hee-haw.

Donkeys generally are identified by their ears, which are larger than those of a horse. They wear their coarse manes clipped and short or shaved close to the neck and come in a variety of sizes from a thirty-six-inch miniature to an elegant Mammoth Jackstock, which is at least fourteen hands (about fifty-six inches) and up. Donkeys may be saddled and harnessed, but they tend to be more laid back in nature. Their voices are raspy and they say aw-ee-aw-ee! They will sound off at any opportunity!

WHEN: Weekend after Labor Day
WHERE: Ozark Empire Fairgrounds, Springfield
NEARBY ATTRACTION: Missouri State University
INFO: 417-833-2660; www.ozarkmountainmuledays.com

38. BACK TO 1855

The year 1855 might have been good for some, but life just before the Civil War on Lake Jacomo, a border town where battles took place, wasn't as peaceful and serene as it's sometimes portrayed.

Missouri Town 1855 is a living history village/museum situated at Lee's Summit and host to the annual FALL FESTIVAL. In 1865, thirty acres of green space was created around original buildings dating from 1821 to 1860. The town's creation followed a master plan that included a school-house, an antebellum home, a settler's cabin, a church, and a tavern—all authentically reproduced to transport the observer back in time. Costumed craftsmen busily go about their tasks and village orators deliver entertaining, long-winded speeches that often make onlookers roar. Their conversations are in character, adding to the festival's realism.

The festival provides the ideal backdrop for visiting Lee's Summit at a time when October foliage bursts into color on the hillsides. The senses are awash with the smell of burning fires and hearty stews cooking in the kettles. Agricultural events staged to the era include hog-calling and the ever-unique "wife calling." A satisfying find—and a real treat from the Civil War era—is the homemade root beer served up in glass bottles and icy cold from the first swallow.

The setting includes period music against a backdrop of beautiful grounds suitable for a picnic. There is a little side fun to be had as well with the watermelon-seed spitting contest.

WHEN: First weekend in October
WHERE: 8010 E. Park Road, Lee's Summit
NEARBY ATTRACTIONS: National Trails, museum
INFO: www.visitmo.com/listing; www.lstourism.com

39. TO MARKET, TO MARKET!

Missourians do so many things well. We boast skilled craftsmen, cooks, gardeners, farmers, entertainers, and even writers. An amazing group of them are on display during the BEST OF MISSOURI MARKET in St. Louis, a celebration of the Show Me State's many talents.

The site of the market, and one of St. Louis's landmark locations, is the Missouri Botanical Garden, known worldwide for its beautiful gardens spread out across seventy-nine acres. Founded in 1859, it holds the title of the nation's oldest botanical garden in continuous operation and is a national landmark that lives up to its mission statement: "To discover and share knowledge about plants and their environment, in order to preserve and enrich life."

The whole family will want to visit the Missouri Market, because there is something for all ages. The biggest find, perhaps, is the collection of 120 Missouri vendors specifically chosen to represent the best in their field. Crafts include items like original jewelry, woodworking, basket making, quilting, live and dried flower arrangements, instrument making, baking, and pottery.

Demonstrations typically draw a crowd, and children in particular love the cow milking, pumpkin decorating, and live farm-animal petting. Local Missouri musicians perform throughout the weekend.

WHEN: First weekend in October
WHERE: Missouri Botanical Gardens, St. Louis
NEARBY ATTRACTION: The Historic Shaw Art Fair, just around the corner
INFO: 314-577-9400; 800-642-8842; www.mobot.org

40. Festive First Families

Marshfield, located in Webster County, was named by its founders for the great American statesman Daniel Webster, who made his home in Marshfield, Massachussets. This historic community holds a three-day event each year called the CHERRY BLOSSOM FESTIVAL. Cherry blossoms do indeed bloom there, but the festival has more to do with the cherry tree that our first president George Washington cut down when he was six years old. As the story goes, when Washington's father first approached him, he replied, "I cannot tell a lie, Pa. I cut it with my hatchet." Legend or fact, the story has been held up as an iconic example of honesty to generations of schoolchildren.

The Cherry Blossom Festival began in 2003 and focuses on celebrating presidential history, as well as the families that have given support to the leaders of our country. One of the best examples of honoring worthy Missourians, and one of the festival's great finds, is the Missouri Walk of Fame. In the spirit of the famous celebrity walk on Hollywood Boulevard and Vine Street, Marshfield's version honors special Missourians and stars by setting their names in stone. The new additions are unveiled each year during the festival.

The event's major centerpiece revolves around Edwin P. Hubble, the Marshfield native and noted astronomer best known for the space telescope that bears his name. The Hubble media event includes a reception and dinner, during which a cherry medal is awarded to a presidential descendant who has displayed sincere service to his family.

In 2006, the festival welcomed the largest gathering of presidential relatives in the nation at a First Families Library dedication. Educational opportunities abound during the festival, with a focus on presidential education. During the First Lady's Breakfast and Presidential Forum, descendants share their relationships with a particular president. Book signings are held, and the event has attracted presidential authors like Margaret Truman. Of course, as the name implies, cherry pies are the festival's sweetest treats, and the event includes a pie contest and a ceremony in which Little Miss and Mr. Cherry Blossom are named.

WHEN: Third weekend in May
WHERE: Courthouse Square, Marshfield
NEARBY ATTRACTION: Lady Bird Johnson Memorial Garden
INFO: www.cherryblossomfest.com; www.marshfieldmochamberofcommerce.com

41. Smell and Taste

Arrow Rock earned its name from the Native Americans who frequently found arrowheads in a part of the town now known as Arrow Rock bluff, a flint-bearing limestone formation that supplied indigenous cultures with raw materials for tools and weapons for thousands of years.

The region, settled in 1829, also earned a mention in the journals of Louisiana Purchase explorers Lewis and Clark and was the home of several notable Missourians, including Dr. John Sappington, who perfected quinine as a treatment for malaria. Arrow Rock's oldest structure is a tavern built in 1834 by Joseph Huston. All of that history helps provide a rich backdrop for the annual SPRING GARDEN SHOW AND TASTE OF MISSOURI, held each May.

At the dawn of spring, the grounds of the historic schoolhouse host the many garden vendors who come to sell plants, garden decor, patio furniture, and home improvement products. Vendors gather inside the school to display crafts and offer tastes of native Missouri foods, including the state's exceptional fruits and vegetables. Tourism officials also are on hand promoting other Missouri attractions.

A real find at this "taste and share" event is the George Caleb Bingham Art Festival, named for the noted artist whose paintings illustrated commerce and life on the Missouri River. Bingham, born in 1811, had by the time of his death in 1879 come to be regarded as the first truly outstanding artist of the American West. His work, along with other artwork, can be found on the tavern lawn during the festival weekend.

WHEN: First weekend in May
WHERE: Stalberg-Jackson Community Center, Arrow Rock
NEARBY ATTRACTION: Lyceum Theatre
INFO: 660-837-3469; www.arrowrock.org

42. A Lot to Sing About

There's always a happy note to be sung in Lebanon, home to one of the state's best musical events. The ANNUAL BRUMLEY GOSPEL SING represents a forty-three-year-old tradition centered around wholesome family entertainment and outstanding song.

More than thirty thousand visitors fuel up and travel to Lebanon each summer to hear their favorite gospel singers at the Cowan Civic Center, host venue for the four-day event. Six concerts feature the "best of the best" singers, many of whom have performed at the Grand Ole Opry.

Gospel sing founder Albert E. Brumley, inducted into the Gospel Hall of Fame in 1972, is best known for songs such as "I'll Fly Away," "Turn Your Radio On," and "I'll Meet You in the Morning." Following Brumley's death in 1977, his son Bob assumed control of the event, which has earned the title of Grand Daddy of Gospel Sings.

In addition to abundant gospel singing, you'll find plenty of pickin' and comedy, including acoustic numbers and evening and matinee performances offered at very affordable prices. The sing brings together fifth and sixth generations of families, many of which plan reunions to coincide with the event.

Lebanon is a historic, charming town founded in 1849 when the railroad was king. It remained on the map thanks to Route 66, which runs through the heart of the town and whom made Lebanon a popular stop among motorists.

WHEN: First weekend in August
WHERE: Cowan Civic Center Exhibition Hall, Lebanon
NEARBY ATTRACTION: Route 66 Museum
INFO: 800-435-3725; www.brumleymusic.com; www.lebanonmissouri.org

43. Have a Shakesperience

Many communities attempt to broaden their cultural offerings by presenting the plays and poetry of William Shakespeare to residents. Perhaps none does it better and more completely than the Shakespeare Studio in Kansas City. Numerous educational opportunities are offered; however, the highlight of the studio's work is the HEART OF AMERICA SHAKESPEARE FESTIVAL in Southmoreland Park each summer.

Open-seating admission to this popular event is free, with spots offered on a first-come, first-served basis on the lush, green hills surrounding the stage. Reserved seating nearer the stage for chairs and blankets is available for twenty dollars.

The festival's mission is to mount a Shakespearean production each summer, and its plays have been seen by more than 470,000 visitors. "Team Shakespeare," the festival's teen performing troupe, is among the many attractions.

Dining at the festival is delicious, clever, creative, and romantic. You can pack your own picnic food and beverage or purchase a box lunch. If you prefer lunch indoors, a multi-course buffet is available. A special VIP tent hosted by Bard's Brio Tuscan Grille is open only prior to performances.

While the subject is Shakespeare and his timeless plays, festival organizers fully embrace twenty-first-century technology such as blogging and multimedia formats, which are available on the festival website.

WHEN: Weekends in June and July
WHERE: Southmoreland Park, Kansas City
NEARBY ATTRACTION: Country Club Plaza
INFO: 816-531-7728; www.kcshakes.org

44. Fiesta Fun!

Florissant opens its arms to friends and families of its Hispanic community during the city's annual HISPANIC FESTIVAL each June.

The St. Louis region boasts a growing Hispanic population centered around new neighborhoods, new businesses, and new entertainment venues. The festival offers an opportunity to celebrate Hispanic culture and heritage alive with an event highlighted by music, authentic crafts, and outstanding food.

First, the food is delicious. The menu includes empanadas made in the authentic Argentine style, tacos and tamales made by Mexican families, and melt-in-your-mouth Bolivian shish kabobs. All of these delicacies can be washed down with a refreshing margarita or a cold beer.

Entertainment offerings include folkloric dancers, children's performances, and clever arts and crafts—all with an eye toward sustaining Hispanic roots and traditions at a time when many U.S.-born Hispanic children are being Americanized in their schools and other activities. Every Latin American country is represented. This festival is one of three Hispanic events held throughout the year in Florissant.

WHEN: Last weekend in June
WHERE: Knights of Columbus Park, Florissant
NEARBY ATTRACTION: Old St. Ferdinand Shrine
INFO: 314-837-6100; www.hispanicfestival.com

45. Poetry in Motion

Montserrat, population two hundred, earned its spot on the world map during the 1904 World's Fair when two trains collided along a stretch of tracks now known as "Dead Man's Curve."

Today, Montserrat is perhaps better known for a cultural event called the MONTSERRAT POETRY FESTIVAL, sponsored by KMOS-TV. Held at Montserrat Vineyards, the free event lends itself to good wine, music, and verse in an outdoor setting beneath a covered pavilion where attendees are free to come and go as they please. Snacks and light meals are available, so visitors can spend the whole day if they choose. The festival kicks off early in the morning and finishes in the evening.

An extensive list of poets from all parts of the country attends, including Missouri's first poet laureate. Most of the poets are published and arrive with impressive resumes. The Cowboy Poet Association sends a representative who is certain to intrigue listeners with real-life experiences. During the presentations, pleasant, non-intrusive music is played, adding to the atmosphere.

As a backdrop to the verse, the vineyards offer breathtaking views of the surrounding hillside, and its location on the northern point of Bristle Ridge provides a panoramic view from east to west. This location was used as a lookout point during the Civil War, and today the hills are marked by neat rows of grapes destined to be pressed into native Missouri wine.

The festival provides a romantic, open-air departure from the usual stuffy, urban library setting.

WHEN: First Saturday in May
WHERE: Montserrat Vineyards, Montserrat
NEARBY ATTRACTION: Blind Boone Park, Warrensburg
INFO: 660-747-0466; www.kmos.org

46. See What's Booming

If you want to have a booming good time in the middle of your summer, visit Joplin. Folks there pull out all the stops to celebrate BOOMTOWN DAYS at Landreth Park, an event that traces its origins to a humble main street festival for the arts but has grown into one of the Midwest's most significant festivals. More than two hundred volunteers from all walks of life and organizations work year-round to create a festive venue for all ages.

Sponsored by the Freedom Now Committee, Boomtown Days is dominated by the can't-miss combination of music and food, including a Tour the World Food Court offering something to satisfy any ethnic appetite as well as American food like turkey legs and hamburgers. The Battle of the Bands is a daylong competition culminating with an evening concert at the amphitheatre that draws huge audiences for such well-known national touring acts as Kansas and .38 Special.

A nominal admission charge allows visitors entry to the park and covers all entertainment and activities, with the exception of food and drink. An incredible fireworks display takes place at dusk.

For a unique perspective of the festival, take one of the helicopter rides that also provides a fifteen-minute tour of Joplin, known as the temporary home to notorious early twentieth-century villains Bonnie and Clyde. Tethered balloon rides also are available. Both the helicopter and balloon rides are weather permitting.

Joplin's slogan claims the city is "where the Midwest is all at its very best," and it's hard to argue with that during Boomtown Days.

WHEN: Second week in June
WHERE: Landreth Park, Joplin
NEARBY ATTRACTION: Route 66 and Frisco Greenway Trail
INFO: 800-657-2534; www.boomtowndays.com; www.visitjoplinmo.com

47. ALL AROUND THE WORLD

You, too, can take a trip around the world—in just one day, no less—at the FESTIVAL OF NATIONS, held in historic Tower Grove Park in St. Louis. A gift to the citizens of St. Louis by Henry Shaw in 1868, the park remains a showcase for the city and the site of one of its more popular and diverse events.

The Festival of Nations is sponsored by the International Institute, a non-profit agency that helps refugees and immigrants gain independence by learning English and overcoming language barriers. The agency also provides contacts to assist with employment, serving more than eight thousand new American citizens each year.

The festival, offering free admission, was created as an annual event to help reunite people with family and friends and celebrate their heritage. Highlights include marketplaces for food and crafts from countries around the world. Entertainment in the form of music and traditional dance provides the backdrop to a unique dining experience.

The educational offerings are something adults as well as children may take advantage of, as not even a world history class could compare to the experience this visual and hands-on event provides. The Worldways Children's Museum offers a fun and unusual feature in which visitors may model fashions from around the world

WHEN: Last weekend in August
WHERE: Tower Grove Park, St. Louis
NEARBY ATTRACTION: Missouri Botanical Garden
INFO: 314-773-9090, ext. 189; www.iistl.org

and learn the customs of various nations. In the diversity circle, adults who wish to meet face-to-face with representatives from different countries may engage in interesting conversation and share their native languages.

Diversity is alive and well in Missouri, particularly at the Festival of Nations.

48. Isesaki Japan Helps Celebrate

You might be unaware that the Sister City to Springfield is Isesaki, Japan, which is why visitors and performers travel each year to the JAPANESE FALL FESTIVAL at the scenic Mizumoto Japanese Stroll Garden in Nathaniel Green Park.

The seven-and-a-half-acre garden's massive beauty unfolds as you follow a stepping-stone path that winds around ponds and amazing rocks, key elements to the Japanese garden's artistry. In Japan, rocks are viewed with respect attributed to the country's history and the topography of its mountains and countryside. The garden reflects the environment of the season and Japan's culture.

The festival garden proudly captures beauty, entertainment, and class, with performers from Japan staging folk dancing as well as other traditional styles. A selection of crafts, made locally or in Japan, is available for purchase. Children tend to migrate to the hands-on projects available at several festival venues, while adults might find the candlelight walk to provide a romantic interlude. Martial arts demonstrations also are held.

Here is a real festival find—the lakeside ceremony held at the "Tea House" features tea-making in an Asian tradition known as Sado, or "the way of the tea." The process involves the ceremonial preparation and serving of green powdered tea, during which visitors may wait on a nearby bench until summoned by the host. Guests may choose between a light, simple meal or a full-course meal, and may wear traditional kimonos. After being served the meal, visitors are returned to wait at the tea house.

WHEN: Weekend after Labor Day
WHERE: Nathaniel Greene Park, Springfield
NEARBY ATTRACTION: Directly east of Horton-Smith Golf Course
INFO: 417-891-1654; 417-864-1049; www.springfieldmo.gov

49. A State of Affairs

The best of rural Missouri can be found at the MISSOURI STATE FAIR in Sedalia, a first-class family fair that takes place on a sprawling 396-acre tract. Over eleven days, the event combines every imaginable hobby and interest among residents of the Show Me State with a nod to the important role rural living plays in our quality of life.

Whether you care to learn more about lawn-care maintenance or hone your hunting and fishing techniques, more than eighteen buildings house fairgoers and offer educational opportunities as well as tents for professional entertainment. Free demonstrations and exhibits highlight the state's latest agricultural innovations.

Recently, the most popular find has been the fair's "going green" component, embodied in the Show Me Green exhibit at the MEC building. Show Me Green encourages visitors to do their part in making sound environmental decisions, and environmental experts demonstrate the latest discoveries in conservation and explain the strategies that fair organizers have adopted in their commitment to making the event greener in future years.

The slogan of the oldest such event in Missouri, dating to 1901, is "preserving, improving, and perpetuating the rich heritage of the Missouri State Fair for generations to come." The well-organized fair continues to grow in size and attendance.

WHEN: Third weekend in August
WHERE: State Fairgrounds, Sedalia
NEARBY ATTRACTION: Bothwell Lodge
INFO: 800-422-3247; 660-827-8150; www.mostatefair.com

50. Nostalgia on Wheels

Historic Cole Camp was the site of an early skirmish during the Civil War, and a section of the town called "Old Clabbertown" still is home to original structures from that era. But its ties to a nineteenth-century national conflict aren't the only attraction in Cole Camp, where in 2000 the late local wood-carver and merchant Jim Maxwell started a clever, unique event centered around his interest in antiques, particularly classic and antique bicycles.

Even after its namesake's death, the JIM MAXWELL ANTIQUE BICYCLE SHOW remains a popular event, drawing bicycle enthusiasts from around the region to ride the "Butterfield Trail." Forty to fifty riders dress in costume to match the era of the bicycle they are riding. The bikes range in vintage from late 1800s "high wheelers" to sleeker, more modern cycles from the 1970s. Children may join the fun and are permitted to ride bicycles of their choice.

The tour's best find is that it traditionally is led by Cole Camp's police chief, who rides a 1937 vintage police bicycle that Jim Maxwell restored.

The touring bicyclists make six stops along the way to hear lecturers recount the history of Cole Camp. One stop is at a cemetery where a Civil War soldier is buried. A costumed re-enactor there plays the violin to mark the solemnity of the moment. The tour ends at the downtown bandstand where trophies are awarded for best costume, best of show, best restored bicycle, best original bicycle, and, occasionally, oldest cyclist.

Through the efforts of Jim's wife, Margie, the event continues to flourish and to provide enjoyment for the whole community.

WHEN: Last Saturday in September
WHERE: On the grounds of the Cole Camp Museum, Cole Camp
NEARBY ATTRACTION: Steam and Tractor Show on Highway 52
INFO: 660-668-2295; www.colecamp.com

51. The Craving of the Fish

Nixa, population twelve thousand, stakes its claim as "Crossroads of the Ozarks" and is a uniquely named town with an unusual event called SUCKER DAYS.

A sucker is a long, brownish fish that can grow to lengths of thirty to ninety inches and has a distinctive dorsal structure that takes the form of a sucker-like organ. Suckers sometimes attach themselves to objects such as small boats.

In recognition of these strange-looking creatures, Sucker Days was founded in the 1950s by Finis Gold. Townspeople would interrupt their work to grab suckers while they were spawning in shallow waters. Once they caught a "mess" of them with treble hooks, they gathered to hold a fish fry complete with plenty of potatoes to soak up the grease. Sucker Days participants admit that suckers as a delicacy are an acquired taste.

Local anglers donate their catches to meet demand for the fish during Sucker Days, for which schools close so that all available hands can help prepare meals for thousands of visitors.

Accompanying the feast are a parade, a carnival, and a variety of music.

WHEN: Third weekend in May
WHERE: Downtown Nixa
NEARBY ATTRACTION: Nixa City Park
INFO: 417-725-1545; www.nixa.com

52. Ozark Highlands Music Culture

Historic West Plains is the perfect place to enjoy and reflect on the music and culture of the Ozark Highlands, and that all comes together each year at the OLD TIME MUSIC OZARK HERITAGE FESTIVAL.

Bluegrass and old-time country music have a different sound than their rural counterparts, and the traditional flavor of the Ozark Southern community attracts musicians, storytellers, and artisans from all over the country. Dancing, fiddling, jigging, and gospel-singing performances and demonstrations are among the festival's highlights, along with a craft component that includes traditional basket making, spinning, blacksmithing, and log skidding.

The festival's organizers are diligent about observing the event's central themes—acknowledging local performers, sustaining and cherishing the expressive traditions, and maintaining a focus on authenticity.

Competition is healthy and lively, so you'll find the Old Time Jig Dance Contest entertaining and enlightening for all age groups. Divisions include ages seventeen and under, eighteen to fifty, fifty-one to seventy, and over seventy. The old timers can put some of the younger contestants to shame thanks to a lifetime of jigging experience. More than one thousand dollars in prizes is handed out, and the contest has gained national notoriety. Other attractions include various workshops, hoedown square dancing, and a quilt show.

Ever wonder what was cooking in a typical nineteenth-century Ozark Kitchen? How about squirrel pot pie, pierogies and sauerkraut, green tomatoes, fried chicken, and homemade bread and cakes—all tastes from the past that are just as scrumptious today.

Kudos to the West Plains Chamber of Commerce, Missouri University-West Plains, the City of West Plains, and the West Plains Arts Council for staging such a quality festival.

WHEN: Third weekend in July
WHERE: Historic downtown West Plains
NEARBY ATTRACTION: The Harlin Museum
INFO: 417-256-4433; www.oldtimemusic.org

53. A Stomping Good Time

Grapes and the fall season go together like salt and pepper, and in Hollister grape harvesting is important enough to be a part of the town's history books.

Generations of local grape growers have brought their grapes to town to be shipped out by rail, and their efforts are celebrated at Hollister's annual GRAPE AND FALL FESTIVAL, which is sponsored by the local chamber of commerce.

Each year, organizers choose a theme, and festival participants dress the part for the festivities, which include wine tasting, great music, a crafts sale, and plenty of delicious food. Admission is free to the festival, and fun-loving visitors can enter the grape stomp for twenty-five dollars per team. Everything takes place on the Grape Stomp Stage downtown at 2 p.m. on the Saturday afternoon of the festival. Teams dress in costumes and bring a CD of their choice of music. The team with the best moves, originality, outrageous style, and costumes wins the stomp competition. Participants are required to stomp for two minutes, and the winner receives the traditional "ugly monkey grape stomping" trophy.

WHEN: Last weekend in September
WHERE: Historic downtown Hollister
NEARBY ATTRACTION: Branson
INFO: 417-334-3050; www.hollisterchamber.net

54. The Best of the Blues

Persimmon Hill Berry Farm in Lampe offers some of the best blueberries Missouri has to offer. This berry, fruit, and mushroom farm is situated in close proximity to scenic Table Rock Lake country in southwest Missouri.

In 1982, Ernie and Martha Bohner started the farm on only two acres of vacant fields and planted blueberries alongside hives of honeybees for pollination. Their hard work led to growth and expansion that has produced what is now a place where families can tote buckets and pick blueberries to their hearts' content.

Fittingly, Lampe's annual PERSIMMON HILL BLUEBERRY FESTIVAL AND MUSIC FEST takes place when the berries are at their peak, and bluegrass music fills the air as activities revolve around the creative ways to prepare food containing the farm's signature crop.

The Cobbler Contest, benefitting the Lives Under Construction Boys Ranch, is a find that is not to be missed. After the judging takes place, the cobblers become part of the benefit's dessert offerings. Contestants are given a free pound of blueberries by noon and must prepare and deliver their entry for judging by 1 p.m. The winner receives a unique, handmade pottery cobbler dish.

Plenty of free activities are available, including tours of the farm, free berry recipes, and tasty berry dessert samples. Nutty Blue Goose Jam is among the favorites, made with blueberries and walnuts.

Should you believe one cannot live on dessert alone, try a sandwich featuring the farm's award-winning barbeque sauce.

WHEN: First Saturday in June
WHERE: Persimmon Hill Farm, Lampe
NEARBY ATTRACTIONS: The Roy Rodgers and Dale Evans Museum
INFO: www.persimmonhill.com

55. All Things Oz

The family music classic *Wizard of Oz* might be seventy-plus years old, but the city of Poplar Bluff celebrates its magical themes at the annual OZ FESTIVAL. The city pulls out all the stops to create this event, which originally was held downtown but now has expanded and moved to Ray Clinton Park.

A different character from Munchkin Land is featured in areas throughout the park, and the visual experience includes a Lion section, a Scarecrow section, a Tin Man section, and a Dorothy section. In the Pageant section, great competitions result in the awarding of crowns for such titles as Miss Ruby Slippers, Miss Munchkin, and Miss Yellow Brick Road, to name a few.

Attendees to the event enjoy dressing in character to compete in the ever-popular and attention-getting costume contest. The parade, complete with favorite characters from the movie, is sure to transport you back to your childhood. And the sounds are perhaps the best find of all, with Oz Karaoke attracting singers eager to take a stab at "Over the Rainbow" and "If I Only Had a Brain." If you can cackle, the Wicked Witch Contest is for you! Vendors offer a variety of familiar Oz-themed trinkets, and a Farmer's Market is open throughout the festival.

Poplar Bluff, a light industrial community nestled in the Ozark foothills, is, for one weekend at least, the destination at the end of the Yellow Brick Road.

WHEN: Second Saturday in June
WHERE: Ray Clinton Park, Poplar Bluff
NEARBY ATTRACTION: Black River Coliseum
INFO: 573-785-7761; www.downtownpoplarbluff.com

56. CELEBRATING CHINA

If you would like to experience Chinese culture without having to buy a ticket to China, visit CHINESE CULTURE DAYS in St. Louis. The city's Missouri Botanical Garden, a seventy-nine-acre venue that is one of the oldest botanical institutions in the United States, serves as the perfect setting for this elegant event.

The festival opens with a grand, colorful parade that includes a seventy-foot dancing dragon, followed by opening ceremonies at Cohen Amphitheater. This exotic celebration offers something for everyone, beginning with a "tea tasting" with traditional musical chimes, that runs during both days of the event. A full tour of the gardens is a must and includes the opportunity to see folk dancing, aerobatics, and lion and dragon dancing at several stops. A pleasantly surprising find is the new Shanghai Acrobatic Circus, where acrobats perform amazing feats of balance and daring.

Other highlights include cooking demonstrations, T'ai Chi instruction, and a fashion and cultural show at Schoenberg Theater that offers the perfect respite for those who need to give their feet a rest.

WHEN: Third weekend in May
WHERE: Missouri Botanical Garden, St. Louis
NEARBY ATTRACTION: Earth Day on the same day in Forest Park
INFO: 800-642-8842; www.mobot.org

The organizers of this event add a few surprises every year with an eye toward their goal of celebrating unity through diversity.

57. Dancing in the Streets

When Patty Robinson, economic development director of Warrenton, managed to secure a grant to provide gaslights for the city, officials decided to celebrate the beauty of these new signature pieces of their downtown. Thus began CATCH THE GLOW ON MAIN STREET, originally organized by the Downtown Merchants Association and now run by city of Warrenton employees.

The event begins with a 5K run/walk at 8 a.m., starting at the downtown courthouse. Top finishers in six or more divisions are awarded gold, silver, and bronze medals. Main Street closes to accommodate music on two stages, and local restaurateurs look forward to this event as an opportunity to move their tables and chairs outdoors to ensure patrons won't miss any of the activities.

Perhaps the most anticipated find is street dancing, which can take place on an impromptu basis among those moved by the sounds of a rotating set of bands. Children's activities include a popular Soap Box Derby down Main Street, and the Classic Car and Motorcycle Show is another must-see. Of course, everyone sticks around until dusk to catch the glow of the lights, the festival's central theme and a source of civic pride for Warrenton.

WHEN: Last Saturday in June
WHERE: Downtown Warrenton, Missouri
NEARBY ATTRACTIONS: County courthouse and Brinkley Park
INFO: 636-456-3535; www.warrenton-mo.org

58. PATCHWORK OF FUN

When you hear the word *Amish*, you probably think of black buggies, scenic farmland, women and girls in bonnets, home-canned food, friendship bread, and most of all, their exceptional quilts.

The Amish of Jamesport didn't settle in the town until 1953, but like others of their faith around the country they built communities based on the belief that their lives should be ruled by Biblical law, not man's. They looked for lush farmland like that in Jamesport, frowning on technology and instead relying on horses, primitive tools, and hand labor to till the land and produce what they needed to survive.

In typical Amish enclaves, women spend their days caring for their children, cooking, and making quilts. Their quilt making caught the attention of the worldwide quilt market with their simplistic yet beautiful style and colors. Black with bold, solid colors was the signature look until recent years, when they adapted to other fabric trends.

Jamesport's ANNUAL AMISH QUILT AUCTION celebrates their unique skill and attracts bidders from many states. Quilts are brought in on consignment from a variety of Amish and English quilters, and a percentage of sales goes towards the betterment of Jamesport. Standing-room-only crowds typically are on hand to see more than one hundred quilts auctioned, with total sales approaching fifty thousand dollars.

This quaint auction has some other fascinating finds, including the opportunity to stay in an Amish home, visit a broom-maker, try out a homemade rocking chair, stay in one of the many historic bed and breakfasts, or purchase handmade Amish bonnets or sugar cookies.

WHEN: Second Saturday in October
WHERE: A.V. Spillman Theater, Jamesport
NEARBY ATTRACTION: Harris Log Cabin in the city park
INFO: 660-684-6146; www.jamesportmo.org

59. A Church Picnic for All

When Perryville, a town of only 7,600 residents, transforms into the host of an event drawing more than 50,000 visitors, it's worth checking out what all the fuss is over. Turns out it's the ANNUAL ST. VINCENT DE PAUL SEMINARY PICNIC. The picnic takes place on five acres of picnic ground surrounded by thirty-six acres of parking, which gives you some idea of the scope of this popular event. This unusual picnic is sponsored by the St. Vincent de Paul Parish, which relies on the herculean efforts of its membership.

The main draw is delicious homemade food like country-kettle-cooked chicken and dumplings and a variety of homemade pies all served buffet style by church workers. Quality live entertainment, as well as the ever-popular bingo games, are among the event's favorite attractions, and a variety of handmade quilts are awarded to lucky bingo winners.

One of the picnic's highlights is a restored 1905 carousel that has delighted generations of visitors. Manufactured by New York–based Hershey-Spellman Co., it is one of many the company has produced and delivered to St. Louis, Eureka, Branson, and Independence, many of which are listed on the National Classic Carousel Census.

The nostalgic "Country Fair" carousel in Perryville has curled front and rear legs outstretched on the horses, which are called jumpers. The horses rock and move from side to side instead of up and down while a small organ plays music in the background.

The picnic regularly attracts alums from the area, as well as many who grew up in Perry County. It is a tradition that has endured for more than one hundred years as a place "where friends meet from everywhere."

WHEN: First weekend in August
WHERE: Seminary Grove on T Road, Perryville
NEARBY ATTRACTION: National Shrine of Our Lady of the Miraculous Medal
INFO: 573-547-4591; www.perryvillemo.com

60. Come Fly Away

Powell Gardens in the small community of Kingsville is a stunningly beautiful, 915-acre tract of rolling hills and gardens that incorporates a nature trail, interesting architecture, and special events like the FESTIVAL OF BUTTERFLIES. Interact in the garden's observatory with hundreds of butterflies, including native species like Blue Morpho, Gulf Fritillary, Mexican Blue Wing, and others. Special exhibits include the Monarch Watch, as well as butterfly plants and Iris varieties that are available for sale.

Children are endlessly fascinated with butterflies, and if they belong to the Powell Gardens Kids Club, they can join their parents at the Soar Like a Butterfly event, where they receive a t-shirt, button, newsletter, discounts, and a free drink at Cafe Thyme.

A little-known find with plenty of appeal is the two-hour photo experience free of outside interruptions, allowing visitors the chance to get special shots of nature's beauty. Some refer to this as a class that can

help you learn and observe basic and advanced photographic techniques, and it provides the privacy to enable those of all skill levels to feel comfortable. A nominal admission charge is required, but the rewards are bountiful and beautiful!

WHEN: Two weekends in mid-August
WHERE: Powell Gardens, Kingsville
NEARBY ATTRACTION: City of Lone Jack, the historic Civil War battle site
INFO: 816-697-2600; www.powellgardens.org

61. Scot or Not

The KANSAS CITY SCOTTISH HIGHLAND GAMES in Riverside introduces visitors to a wee bit of Scotland in every possible way, and the very green grass of the E.H. Young Park is the perfect venue for the event.

In accordance with Scottish tradition, sanctioned heavy athletes compete for championships in a variety of weight divisions. Live Scottish livestock exhibits provide the opportunity to get a close-up look at Clydesdale horses, sheep dogs, and Highland cattle. Food vendors offer authentic tastes of traditional dishes from Scotland and the British Isles, and fly-fishing events are designed for youthful anglers.

Music fills the air with bagpipe and drum performances, and harpists of all ages play at the Harp Tent during both days of the festival. Among Scottish instruments, the Celtic harp is second in recognition only to bagpipes, and here the audience can enjoy hands-on experience with these fascinating instruments. Performances by Celtic storytellers and pipe and drum demonstrations are aimed for children.

The Scottish Clan's Torchlight Ceremony in E.H. Young Park's amphitheatre honors a Scottish clan at each festival. To learn whether there is some Scot in your background, visit each clan's tent and check to see if your family name is listed. Each clan has a unique tartan plaid that its members proudly wear while sharing their history with visitors.

WHEN: Second weekend in June
WHERE: E.H. Young Park, Riverside
NEARBY ATTRACTION: Argosy Casino Hotel and Spa
INFO: www.kcscottishgames.org

62. A Crafty Weekend

In 1978, twelve crafters started a small event called the FAIR GROVE HERITAGE REUNION on the town square and in a vacant building in tiny Fair Grove, population one thousand.

Over the years the reunion grew from within and without, attracting additional crafters as well as purveyors of local pastries and produce while enjoying increased participation from local residents. Today, more than three hundred crafters participate in what has become a two-day event that attracts as many as forty thousand people in one day and is sponsored by the Fair Grove Historical Society.

An event-filled day begins with the can't-miss 8:45 a.m. church service, affording the chance to see the sun peek over the Wommack Mill's rooftop for an unforgettable and relaxing sight. Wommack Mill becomes a bustling spot with demonstrations of wheat thrashing and steam-powered engines engaged in various tasks.

Seven miles away at the Walnut Springs Farm and Museum, another important part of the reunion plays out. The museum hosts a wagon train that originates there before traveling to Fair Grove, with wagons arriving at the farm the night before to camp out for an early morning departure. There they enjoy a good meal of barbeque, fried steak, beans, and sourdough biscuits. The farm's museum component includes an authentic dairy barn, carriage shop, blacksmith shop, and harness shop. Weekend visitors are apt to see what's advertised as a "country wedding" taking place at one of the barns.

The 420-acre farm was restored and reconstructed by Mike and Cathy Brown and is listed on the National Register of Historic Places.

WHEN: Last weekend in September
WHERE: Fair Grove Square, Fair Grove
NEARBY ATTRACTION: Walnut Springs Farm and Museum
INFO: 417-859-7954; www.fghps.org; www.walnutspringsfarm.com

63. CELEBRATE POLAND

The Polish National Alliance celebrates its heritage nationwide, but nowhere is that celebration bigger or better than in St. Louis, where PNA Nest 45 has held its annual POLISH FESTIVAL each September for more than thirty-five years. Visitors flock to the Polish Falcon Gardens beginning Friday for lunches and dinners offering authentic Polish food, including dishes passed on through generations.

On Saturday, a variety of games begin, and the festival's real find is the Bi-State Polka Dance Contest. This nineteenth-century Bohemian dance became popular in ballrooms across Europe and North and South America, and it remains just as popular now as a folk dance and competitive ballroom dance based on polka's three-steps-and-a-hop-in-double-time foundation.

Contestants are judged on presentation, presence, and polka-dancing ability. Registration is free, and prizes are awarded. Those who catch the polka fever and would like to perform the dance on a regular basis may become members of the St. Louis Metro Polka Club.

The Polish Falcons of America is a non-profit organization segmented into nests or lodges whose original aim was to promote its heritage, regenerate its members in body and spirit, and inspire in Polish-American immigrants a sense of well-being and independence from the fatherland.

January is designated as Polka Month, but the St. Louis Polish Festival ensures that January is not the only month the dance and its heritage are celebrated.

WHEN: First weekend in September
WHERE: Polish Falcon Gardens, St. Louis
NEARBY ATTRACTION: The famous Crown Candy Kitchen
INFO: www.polishfalcons.org

64. Day Dream in the Lily Fields

As you approach the charming little town of Defiance, slow down a bit to get a good look at the stately entrance to Wine Country Garden. Upon entering, the road winds to the top of the hill toward a large colonial home on the left amid twenty-four acres of a beautiful, fully functioning plant nursery. The lush hills beneath the estate are lined with rows of grapes, trees, bushes, and flowers. An inviting, perfectly landscaped lake sits to one side, home to groups of swans and ducks.

Wine Country Garden offers an indoor wine-tasting bar with a tempting menu of lunch delicacies. A complex of multi-level indoor and outdoor patios hosts themed parties throughout summer and fall. And the banquet room with a large, exquisite fireplace regularly hosts weddings on the weekends.

The most visually breathtaking months to visit are June and July, when the 80,000 perennials, trees, and shrubs are in full bloom. That's when Wine Country Garden hosts its annual DAY LILY DAYS, providing eye candy in the form of some 250 varieties of the beautiful flowers.

Three acres of lilies burst out in colors for visitors who may choose between a walking tour and a spin through the fields on a golf cart. Hundreds of potted lilies are available for purchase. Among the best sellers are Firestorm, Mauna Lea, and Prester. An early season coupon goes out to repeat customers, so it's worthwhile to get on the mailing list.

Take it all in as you sip your wine, have some lunch, plan your garden, and view the lilies.

WHEN: June and July
WHERE: Wine Country Garden, Defiance
NEARBY ATTRACTION: Wine country, Augusta
INFO: 636-798-2288; www.winecountrygardens.net

65. Wagons Ho!

Hold your horses Missourians, the CHUCKWAGON RACING track is quite the exciting venue in little Raymondville, population 450. Chuckwagon racing began in 1920 and has grown into an organized sport, with the Midwest Chuckwagon Racing Association credited with bringing races to Missouri, as well as Kansas and Oklahoma.

As many as twenty teams of wagon drivers are supported by sidekicks and riders on horseback. The race starts with a two-man team consisting of a cook (a name for a Western hired hand designated for cooking on the ride), who stands behind the wagon ready to toss a bedroll onto the back, and another team member who has the reins of his horse in one hand and the handle to the cook stove in the other. The object is for the cook to load the bedroll and then hop aboard the wagon.

A pistol shot starts the action, and the team's outrigger tosses his stone onto the wagon before mounting his steed. Racing around an oval track, the outrigger must cross the finish line ahead of the team's wagon. Contestants use a variety of animals, including large and small mules, ponies, and horses. The sport has evolved from a rowdy party atmosphere to a family oriented event.

An unexpected find is the Cowboy Church, started by Cowboys for Christ leader Matt Wagoner, who believed its addition would help the races thrive.

The affordable, all-around fun attracts visitors of all ages and can offer as much excitement as a NASCAR race or a dirt bike ride in the hills.

WHEN: First weekend in August
WHERE: Silver Nickel Arena, Raymondville
NEARBY ATTRACTION: Boiling Springs Resort
INFO: 660-238-2249; www.mcwra.net

66. A Woman's Affair

Caruthersville, located on the banks of the Mississippi River, is a small community that serves as its county seat, and folks there know how to have a good time. The Caruthersville Chamber of Commerce is known for creating clever events that turn into popular, well-attended attractions. Their best efforts might be found in the town's annual WHITE GLOVE GALA, which honors Caruthersville's women.

Men are permitted to take part in an event that is known as "an auction with a twist," but only if they agree to serve as auctioneers, waiters, or cashiers. Prizes range from trips to Disney World to small pieces of jewelry, all of which can be had for as little as one dollar. How, you ask? If you are

interested in bidding on an item, you raise your assigned numbered paddle, and your name goes into a hat for that item.

The winner is chosen immediately. Small items also are auctioned, which may be just a quarter or fifty cents. Specific auction items also are tailored for young ladies who take

WHEN: Third Saturday in April
WHERE: Armory Building, Caruthersville
NEARBY ATTRACTION: Caruthersville Sports Complex
INFO: 573-333-2142; 573-333-1222

part. Each year brings a different theme, and past themes have included "Chocolate Fantasy" and "Mardi Gras." The attire—including everything from fancy ballroom gowns to costumes to pajamas—is at least half the fun.

A highlight of the gala is the auctioned kisses that go out to men from the chamber of commerce. A ten-dollar admission charge covers food, beverages, and entertainment. The first three hundred tickets sell out quickly each year, usually to repeat attendees.

67. Mexican Culture Ignites

Members of St. Joseph's Holy Rosary Parish began celebrating their Mexican heritage in 1931, originally at Holy Rosary School at the behest of Father Maximilian Rupp.

When the school closed, St. Patrick's Parish took over the celebration in 1969 as a fund-raiser, and the ST. PATRICK'S MEXICAN FIESTA was born, exploding in popularity in 1980 into what remains one of the town's most celebrated events.

Traditional dishes like rice and beans, enchiladas, tamales, chicken mole, tacos, and fideo help bring in the crowds. A fiesta favorite is the cascarones, egg shells that have a small portion of the top removed so they can be filled with confetti. Members save their egg shells in cartons to make cascarones, which are popular with adults as well as children. For the younger set, organizers expanded by adding a carnival.

A king and queen are chosen from among contestants ages fourteen to eighteen, while the prince and princess must be between four and eight years old. What follows is the fiesta's best find, a regal Mexican Coronation Dance that attracts generations of kings and queens who have been crowned over the years and return for the opportunity to reunite with family and friends.

WHEN: Last weekend in July
WHERE: Grounds of St. Patrick's Church, St. Joseph
NEARBY ATTRACTION: Pony Express Museum
INFO: 816-279-2594

---

68. Missouri's Dogwood Acknowledged

Everything's blooming in Neosho in the springtime. The city of 10,500 is located on the edge of the Missouri Ozarks, and its name comes from the Indian *Ne-o-zho*, which means clear or abundant water. The nine springs within the city limits lend the town its nickname—"City of Springs."

Another famous tagline for Neosho is "Flower Box City," because of the many flower boxes sprinkled throughout the town. The Neosho Chamber of Commerce has a contest each year to name the most attractive flower box. At Morse Park, a railroad car was converted into a flower box.

WHEN: First Saturday in April
WHERE: Neosho
NEARBY ATTRACTION: Crowder College
INFO: 417-451-1925; www.neoshomo.org

Among the flower boxes are beautiful dogwood trees that serve as the basis for Neosho's ANNUAL DOGWOOD TOUR each April. Six different species of dogwoods are on display, and blooming redbud trees add to the ambiance. The best place to start is Neosho High School, from which visitors can meander throughout a town whose natural beauty has earned it *Look* magazine's "All-American City" distinction.

The real find at this event is a legend that townspeople say began with the Crucifixion, when Jesus ordered that the Dogwood blossom should be in the form of a cross at the edge of each petal. The story held that there should be nail prints, and in the center, a crown of thorns. The tree was to be a reminder of the cross. The Missouri version says the tree is a symbol of divine sacrifice and promotes eternal life.

Neosho's most famous citizen is renowned artist Thomas Hart Benton, who painted a mural that is in the Missouri State Capitol. The work captures his childhood growing up in Neosho.

69. THE BIGGEST AND BEST

St. Charles is a very proud host of the largest craft festival in Missouri, THE FESTIVAL OF THE LITTLE HILLS. The event began in 1971 on historic Main Street, with an original concept in which authentic crafts and period foods were offered in a festival managed by the South Main Preservation Society.

As the festival grew and prospered it changed hands until it reached its current status as a massive celebration that attracts 350,000 visitors and occupies eighteen city blocks from Main Street to Frontier Park on the Missouri River. Buses shuttle visitors to and from every part of the historic town, and crafters come from throughout the country for an event that has earned a reputation as a trendsetter for the future of arts and crafts.

Live entertainment on the Jaycees' outdoor stage features local and international talent, and a children's carnival and rock-climbing venue are popular attractions. Every other year, the amazing Marlin Perkins Animal Kingdom appears with its large giraffe head peering through the roof of the tent. The animals offer an educational component and are perhaps the festival's best find. Food booths are operated by non-profit organizations offering a range of dishes from spicy gumbo to ears of corn on a stick.

The number of antique vendors is growing, adding a historic flavor. The event is extremely well-organized and well-run, helping the festival to easily rank among the ten best attractions in the state each year.

WHEN: Third weekend in August
WHERE: Historic district, St. Charles
NEARBY ATTRACTION: Missouri's first state capitol
INFO: www.festivalofthelittlehills.com; www.historicstcharles.com

70. YOU HAVE A STEAK HERE

Many towns build events around food, and Salisbury is no different. The town hosts its annual SALISBURY STEAK FESTIVAL to celebrate its contribution to the world of dinner fare.

The event starts with a parade and includes basketball and horseshoe tournaments and a tractor pull said to be among the best anywhere, featuring well-known brands like John Deere, Massey-Ferguson, and Farmall. Acceleration control is pivotal to a good pull, and drivers cannot take off too quickly or they risk being disqualified.

But the festival is really about the steak with which the town shares its name. The story behind Salisbury steak, told at the festival's steak supper, begins not with Lucius Salisbury, who founded the town in 1867, but with Dr. James Salisbury, who studied diet and nutrition and advised people to eat beef chased by cups of hot water. He came up with the idea of chopped beef in the late nineteenth century, which later became known as the hamburger, which gained popularity during World War I.

The festival's popular steak dinner is a bargain at five dollars for steak, baked potato, coleslaw, iced tea, and a roll. It is traditionally served with gravy, mashed potatoes, and noodles.

WHEN: First weekend in June
WHERE: Salisbury City Park, Salisbury
NEARBY ATTRACTION: Swan Lake National Wildlife Refuge
INFO: 660-388-6197; 660-388-5984

71. It's Margaritaville

Bearcat Getaway campgrounds on the Black River in Lesterville is a long way from the Gulf of Mexico, but you would never know it when the campgrounds holds its annual PARROT HEAD BEACH PARTY each summer during the first weekend in June.

For nearly ten years now the Parrot Head Club has offered visitors the heat of the sun, delicious margaritas, and the popular sounds of Jimmy Buffett during an event that revels in fun games and contests created to reflect the laid back "Margaritaville" lifestyle.

Buffett, of course, first began playing his unique style of music with songs such as "A White Sport Coat With a Pink Carnation," while performing with the Coral Reefers. His best-selling book, *Tales of Margaritaville*, details his experiences, and the Parrot Head Beach Party brings them to life.

Live entertainment takes the stage both nights, with Naked Cove Entertainment and Landshark Matt on Friday, followed by Phins on Saturday. To complete the theme, campers deck out their sites in beach décor and dress up in island-inspired garb to compete for prizes for best campsite and best costume.

The main event is the Saturday night Luau and Pig Roast where, for twelve dollars per person, diners are treated to a mouthwatering lineup of entrees that includes Oma'opio Imu Roasted Pig, Island Pineapple Chicken, and Mahi Mahi Corn Chowder. If you can hang around until Sunday morning, an all-you-can-eat breakfast is served.

Key West was Jimmy Buffett's home base, but Buffett often says Margaritaville can be anywhere you want it to be—even Lesterville, Missouri.

WHEN: First weekend in June
WHERE: Bearcat Getaway, Lesterville
NEARBY ATTRACTION: Johnson's Shut-ins
INFO: 888-356-2844; 573-637-2264; www.bearcatgetaway.com

72. Arcadia Valley's Gem

One of Missouri's most historical events took place in the valley of Pilot Knob and is commemorated during the BATTLE OF PILOT KNOB RE-ENACTMENT, which recreates the Civil War battle that took place in the vicinity of what is now Pilot Knob, Ironton, and Arcadia.

Fort Davidson, located three hundred yards from Pilot Knob Mountain, was the site of a significant battle in 1864. Confederate troops assaulted Union forces dug in at the earthworks fort, leaving some fifteen hundred soldiers dead or wounded. The fort and battle site are listed on the National Register of Historic Places.

Every third year, a full-scale re-enactment of the battle is staged, attracting thousands of visitors to the valley.

So authentic is the fighting that you can easily lose yourself in the nineteenth century amid the two-day battle that includes the fort's spectacular destruction on Saturday night. Other activities include a re-enactor's ball; infantry, artillery, and cavalry drills; and medical demonstrations from the time period that take place in several buildings, including Immanuel Lutheran Church, which was used as a makeshift hospital during the war.

For history buffs, a special find are the lectures given by Civil War authors, most from Missouri, who provide a timeline and perspective on the events depicted in the re-enactment. Photo opportunities abound, with the beautiful valley offering glimpses of historic buildings and scenic views. Vendors serve delicacies from the mid-1800s, and craftsmen demonstrate some of the artistry of that time.

WHEN: Every four years on the third weekend in September, in 2010 and 2014
WHERE: Arcadia Valley, Pilot Knob
NEARBY ATTRACTION: Iron County Courthouse
INFO: 573-546-7117; www.arcadiavalley.biz/civilwar

73. Seek and Find

More than fifty vendors from Missouri and surrounding states descend upon historic, charming Weston each April for the LIONS CLUB ANTIQUES AND COLLECTIBLES SHOW, an opportunity not only to browse great items but also to take in the town's exceptional architecture.

Sponsored by the Weston Chamber of Commerce and the local Lions Club, the event features everything from fine china to antique jewelry and draws a steady base of clients built up over the past twenty-five years.

The show opens on Friday, and Saturday you'll find a unique opportunity to learn about the antiques and collectibles trade

WHEN: Last weekend in April
WHERE: Weston Burley House, Weston
NEARBY ATTRACTION: Weston Train Depot
INFO: 816-640-2909; 888-635-7457; www.westonmo.com

through an event called Conversations with the Experts. Lunch is offered on the premises, so you can spend the entire day.

The antiques atmosphere is enhanced by the event's venue—the Weston Burley House, where tobacco auctions were held beginning in 1939. Weston had the distinction of being the only tobacco market west of the Mississippi and generated millions of dollars for the local economy. Plenty of tobacco-industry memorabilia is offered for sale, which reminds attendees of the show's connection to the town's tobacco-growing heritage. Proceeds from the admission fee go to various charities.

74. Tango with the Arts

You won't be a square if you attend the NOT SO SQUARE ARTS FESTIVAL—held, appropriately enough, on the town square in Mt. Vernon. For one day, the Mt. Vernon Regional Arts organization hosts a free full day of top-notch art, food, music, and dance.

Artists manning fifty booths offer a variety of artwork suitable for gift-giving to recipients of all ages and for all occasions. The event includes workshops for adults and children to enhance awareness of fine art and writing. If it's entertainment you're seeking, check out the Not so Shakespeare in the Park Players, as well as musical satire and dueling piano players.

The most delightful and entertaining find is the Meet Me in the Middle International Tango Festival, held in conjunction with the arts festival and sponsored by the Missouri Arts Council and the National Endowment of the Arts. Demonstrations by professional performers provide an authentic flavor of Argentina's tango, which endures as a beloved, mystifying dance.

Food-wise, a taste of Mt. Vernon's many delicacies is available throughout the day, along with a farmer's market featuring locally grown produce.

Mt. Vernon is the seat of Lawrence County and the start of scenic Route 265, the Ozark Mountain Parkway.

WHEN: Third Saturday in September
WHERE: Town square, Mt. Vernon
NEARBY ATTRACTION: James Memorial Chapel
INFO: www.mtvernon-cityhall.org

75. A Sportsman's Delight

If you were raised in Missouri, chances are you grew up around the beauty of water, nature, and plentiful sports. All three are celebrated at the annual MISSOURI WATERFOWL FESTIVAL in Kennett, located in Southeast Missouri near the boot heel, an ideal spot to fish, hunt, and hike.

The festival was designed for hunters and outdoor enthusiasts to come together for fun and education, with an emphasis on families. The two-day event is packed with activities that include archery shoots, a duck-calling contest, a children's decoy-painting contest, a 5K run, and a fun Speed Retriever contest open to anyone with a dog. An award goes to the fastest dog to traverse a one hundred-yard obstacle course, retrieve the dummy, and return it to his master waiting at the starting line.

The festival's most curious find is the BB Gun Shoot, which has been known to cause alarm among those who question an event in which children compete with firearms. But rest assured that safety is a top priority, and rules are put into effect to protect contestants. The Daisy Rifle Company serves as sponsor and furnishes Grizzly Pump Air Rifles, numerous targets, pellets, and shooting glasses for the event, which is open to kids ages five to fifteen accompanied by an adult.

Drug dog seminars and other sports and hobby demonstrations underscore the festival's emphasis on sportsman's education. Celebrity sportsmen are a big draw, as well as a Miss Waterfowl Pageant, which adds a touch of beauty to an otherwise rugged, outdoor scene.

WHEN: Third weekend in October
WHERE: Kennett American Legion and Fairgrounds, Kennett
NEARBY ATTRACTION: Sheryl Crow Aquatic Center
INFO: 573-717-0999; www.missouriwaterfowlfestival.com; www.kennettmo.com

76. Christmas at the Mansion

Missourians are quite proud of their Governor's Mansion, and rightly so. Built in 1871, its elegant Renaissance decor has moved many a First Lady to describe it as a "fairytale mansion."

Jefferson City, home of the state capitol, entertains multitudes of guests during the Christmas holiday season. A highlight of the season is the HOLIDAY CANDLELIGHT TOUR, a stunning experience started by First Lady Carolyn Bond. A portrait of Bond in a red formal dress is displayed in the double parlor and, appropriately, serves as the focus of its lavish Christmas decor.

Each room on the mansion tour boasts a Christmas tree displayed against a backdrop featuring its own theme and color. Clusters of poinsettias can be found throughout the mansion and provide great decorating ideas to take home with you, but they aren't the only find. You'll see unusual trimmings like peacock feathers, elaborate ribbons on the themed trees, and garlands of ornaments and greenery displayed on the many mantels throughout the mansion.

At the entrance to the mansion, candlelights set the tone for the holiday tour. The famous winding stairway in the entry serves as the stage for high school choirs that perform on a rotating basis throughout the evening, singing traditional Christmas carols. Costumed docents are stationed in each room, encouraging visitors to take their time to look around, ask questions, and marvel at the beautiful appointments while wondering about who might have lived in the home over the years.

The tour isn't complete without a stop at the small gift shop displaying the mansion's annual custom-designed Christmas ornament.

WHEN: First and second weekends in December
WHERE: Governor's Mansion, Jefferson City
NEARBY ATTRACTION: First state capitol building
INFO: 573-751-2854; www.missourimansion.org

77. COWBOY CULTURE

Mountain View is perhaps best known as the City of Murals, and buildings throughout the town are decorated with art, including one painted to look like a log cabin.

In that vein, the Mountain View Arts Council, an active volunteer organization, sponsors the truly unique MISSOURI COWBOY POETRY FESTIVAL. For more than ten years poets, singers, actors, and storytellers have been bringing their talents to Mountain View for one of the Midwest's largest cowboy poetry and music events. Some thirty performers from five states converge to compete with their original work and have fun with their contemporaries.

There is much to see, learn, and do at the festival, but the best find is Friday's kick-off performances by local students. The evening continues with the Supper with the Cowboys event, a dinner featuring winners from the local school's fifth-grade poetry competition, which is open to the public.

Free performances continue Saturday at the Mountain View Health Care Center, with a grand finale show staged at the Community Center. On Sunday morning, the poets and musicians conclude the event with "Cowboy Church" at Mountain View Methodist Church.

Settled in 1866, Mountain View is situated in the heart of the Ozarks, meaning it's possible to spend part of the day listening to music in the amphitheater and part watching for bald eagles in a beautiful mountainous setting.

WHEN: Last full weekend in April
WHERE: Mountain View Community Center, Mountain View
NEARBY ATTRACTION: Historic Dawt Mill
INFO: www.mountainviewmo.com; www.mountainview.macaa.net

78. The Band Plays On

Best known for its healing, natural mineral spring water, El Dorado Springs has earned a spot on the map for another reason—its annual FOUNDERS DAY PICNIC, which has become a big draw because of its strong musical history.

In 1886, eight young men started a band that remains in existence today and boasts the longest-running, continually used bandstand in the United States. Round with a stone foundation, the bandstand is located in Spring Park and named the Sunderwirth Bandstand, after its founder. There you will find the town's Municipal Band on hand for any and all occasions, including the Founders Day Picnic.

What you might find unusual at this annual, can't-miss event is that it has been designated as a meeting place for class reunions. An average of ten alumni classes meet at each picnic to celebrate the anniversaries of their graduation years.

Live music, featuring both local and Nashville talent, plays on a constructed stage, and the schedule includes fun activities such as a hula-hoop contest, turtle races, and a baby crawl.

Completing the event is the side variety of food booths and a carnival that moves many visitors to suggest the event is "state fair–quality."

WHEN: Weekend nearest July 20
WHERE: Spring Park, El Dorado Springs
NEARBY ATTRACTION: Wayside Museum
INFO: 417-876-4154; 417-876-2691

79. Lights and Santa Delights

Monett earned its status primarily as a Frisco Railroad stop, an association that allowed the town to become a hub of agricultural trade, retail commerce, and small manufacturing during the late-nineteenth and early twentieth centuries. But today folks in Monett also are proud of their annual FESTIVAL OF LIGHTS, a Christmas-themed event that includes more than seventy animated themes lit throughout Monett South Park. Coordinated by the town's chamber of commerce, the displays are sponsored by local businesses.

Starting on November 25, visitors can drive through free of charge to view the displays, or the local Jaycees will pull visitors in a wagon, offering hot chocolate or coffee along the way. The impressive Poinsettia Arch is always a hit, as is the six-seat animated carousel, a display started in 2003 that has grown in size and popularity each year.

A bonus find at the festival is the large Christmas parade down the town's main thoroughfare, Broadway. On the first Saturday in December, Santa leads a procession of floats, bands, and vehicles decorated in unique Christmas style. More than one hundred delightful entries compete for awards, including the ribbon for Best of Show, as well as cash prizes for first, second, and third places.

The community sticks around afterward for festivities that continue throughout the day, including children's visits with Santa. Many of the local churches are open to serve hot refreshments. Stores extend their hours to maximize shopping opportunities for those still completing their Christmas lists, and spirited Christmas music plays throughout the town during the festival.

WHEN: November and December
WHERE: Monett South Park and Broadway, Monett
NEARBY ATTRACTION: Monett's Historical Society
INFO: 417-235-7919; www.kdbsites.com/chamber

---

80. A Native American Happening

When summer fades to fall and with it arrives crisp temperatures and gorgeous foliage, the small town of Blackwater gears up for its annual NATIVE AMERICAN LIVING CULTURE EVENT.

William Branson, a Northern Cree, organizes a colorful, festive experience that draws Native Americans from different states to dance, drum, and sing against the backdrop of a town steeped in history. Blackwater was originally a Native American settlement named after the Blackwater River, which flows nearby.

Branson provides detailed explanations about the town, its history, and the various activities included in the cultural event, one of the highlights of which is an eighteen-foot-tall Cheyenne teepee that helps set the stage for visitors.

Native American–style flute player Sarah Blanton provides music appropriate for the occasion. Little Horse Drum, a Native American drum group, stage performances in full, authentic regalia that routinely entertain hundreds of visitors.

A really cool find are the craft demonstrations of porcupine quillwork and beadwork, which also are available for purchase. Buckshot Trading Co., an authentic, circa 1890s shop, offers additional Native American merchandise, including colorful, heavy wool saddle blankets, rugs, hand-woven baskets, and handmade pottery.

Trading company owner Gerald Cunningham caters to those wishing to dress in period style, guiding visitors through purchases of "living history" clothing that includes calico prairie dresses, hats, mountain-man shirts, and turquoise jewelry.

WHEN: Second Saturday in October
WHERE: Downtown Blackwater
NEARBY ATTRACTION: Arrow Rock
INFO: 660-846-2224; www.blackwater-mo.com

81. A Salty Affair

The BOONSLICK FOLK FESTIVAL in Fayette celebrates the town's early nineteenth-century salt manufacturing industry, which was centered on the saline springs that seep into the valley of Salt Creek. During their exploration, Lewis and Clark described sightings of animals like deer, elk, and bison gathering to lick salt from the deposits along the creek.

The town sprang up in 1805, when Nathan and David Morgan Boone—sons of pioneer woodsman Daniel Boone—discovered the springs and began manufacturing salt at that location. Salt was a valuable commodity in that era, and between 1806 and 1833, the mine was the main salt producer for early settlements along the Missouri River.

WHEN: Labor Day
WHERE: Boonslick State Park, Fayette
NEARBY ATTRACTION: Arrow Rock
INFO: 660-248-2011; 660-248-5246; fayette.missouri.org

The seventeen-acre site, owned and operated by Missouri's Department of Natural Resources, does not have electricity or running water, so the festival takes on a truly primitive feel. Family entertainment centers on simple, yet enjoyable activities like apple bobbling, throwing corncob darts, and stilt walking. Demonstrators display purist crafts such as quilting, spinning, and weaving. Crafters dressed in period costumes provide tours of the grounds.

Not to be missed is the event's best find, in which historians show visitors the location of the salt springs, describe the mining process, and underscore its importance to the region's nineteenth-century economy. Another highlight is the impressive Salt Lake Diorama, on display throughout the festival.

82. Art for the Sky

Since 1972, St. Louis has provided visitors with a unique, healthy "high" at its annual GREAT FOREST PARK BALLOON RACE, a colorful spectacle that draws thousands to the historic park.

The event begins on Friday evening with the Balloon Glow on Central Field in the park, providing breathtaking views of balloons aglow against the backdrop of a twilit sky. During the walk-through from 7 p.m. to 8:30 p.m., visitors can get up close and personal with the balloons. Refreshments are served, and things really light up at 9 p.m. with a fireworks show.

Saturday is race day, with activities starting at noon and continuing until 6:30 p.m. The race begins with the designated lead balloon taking off ahead of some seventy others in pursuit. The one that succeeds in dropping a birdseed baggie closest to the lead balloon wins!

The designs are amazing. The Energizer Bunny balloon is fifteen feet taller than the Statue of Liberty, weighs 1,170 pounds, and is powered by twin burners that keep it aloft with the power of thirty million BTUs.

Other fun attractions include pony rides, games, music, and crafts for all ages, making it a photographer's paradise. Fittingly, a photo contest is held each year in three categories: adult, child, and young adult.

WHEN: Third weekend in September
WHERE: Central Field, Forest Park, St. Louis
NEARBY ATTRACTION: The Jewel Box
INFO: www.greatforestparkballoonrace.com

83. Cotton Picking Time

Agriculture plays a significant role in many Missouri festivals, and Sikeston's annual COTTON CARNIVAL is no different.

Sikeston's claim to fame is as the northernmost producer of cotton in the United States, and the community celebrates that heritage with one of the state's largest parades, featuring the Carnival King and Queen and Little Mr. and Mrs. Cotton Carnival. As many as twelve marching bands participate, coming from all over Southeast Missouri. The event is sponsored by American Legion Post 114 and its auxiliary, and a different theme is chosen every year. Like any good carnival, this one features rides and entertainment for all ages, along with art shows and historic exhibits. A real find at the event is the crowning of Miss Sikeston, a student chosen from among Sikeston Senior High School's population.

Sikeston is located at the top of Missouri's boot heel and has a population of 17,000. The town was founded in 1860 by John Sikes and is home to rich cotton fields and other Midwest produce. According to economic research by the USDA, the region produces 900 to 1,100 pounds of cotton per acre, shattering the misconception that only the "real" Southern states, and not Missouri, are bona fide cotton producers. It is, however, the only part of Missouri that produces cotton.

The Cotton Carnival is timed to take place at the end of the cotton-picking season, giving cotton farmers the chance to celebrate another successful harvest.

WHEN: Last Saturday in September
WHERE: Sikeston Jaycee rodeo grounds, Sikeston
NEARBY ATTRACTION: Lambert's Café
INFO: 573-471-2499; 888-309-6591

84. The Best Little Fair in the Land

The tiny town of Altenburg is a charming community with manicured farms sporting white painted fences, green rolling hills, and well-kept barns. Germans settled in the area because it bore a resemblance to their homeland, and Altenburg's population of 309 residents makes it a quintessential American small town.

The community boasts great schools, a privately owned bank, churches, a winery, eateries, museums, and retail shops and services.

The town earned its spot on the map by hosting the EAST PERRY FAIR, whose quality has brought comparisons with state fairs and earned it the distinction of "the best little fair in the land." Like many fairs, the East Perry event includes 4-H exhibits, crafts, tractor pulls, and livestock, produce, and crafts judging.

A unique and unexpected find is the jumping mule competition, when the animals shed their typically stubborn nature, with a few exceptions, and leap over fences. Normally at least twenty mules compete, specially trained by their owners to jump fences that gradually increase in height until a winner is determined.

The fair's traditional white cheese sandwich is the perfect antidote for the hearty appetite and is made and sold by a local church.

WHEN: Third weekend in September
WHERE: Perry County, I-55, Altenburg
NEARBY ATTRACTION: Tower Rock Winery
INFO: 573-824-5827; www.tower-rock-winery.com/altenburg.htm

85. Celebrating Quilted Art

Quilting has emerged as a huge industry celebrating both the individual artist and America's heritage as a country that produces distinctive and beautiful quilt designs. Shows both large and small, conventions, and markets throughout the world offer varieties of American-produced quilts.

At the heart of some of Missouri's best quilt production is the COUNTRY PATCHWORK QUILT GUILD SHOW in Marshal. Each year, organizers develop a special theme that is followed throughout the show's host venues. Betty Lenz, a longtime quilter and Marshal resident, founded the quilt guild and, along with her friend Faye Kuzza, produced the first show at St. Peter's Catholic Church Hall in 1987. Fourteen years later, they moved it to the local YMCA, which accommodates hundreds of hanging quilts, as well as the hundreds of visitors who attend each year. The guest book proudly displays the names of attendees from no fewer than thirteen states.

Talent abounds among the guild's nearly one hundred members, who include quilt book authors, professional quilt makers, quilt teachers, and quilt collectors. This historic craft remains a unique find these days, with technology trying to meet strong demand.

Visitors may vote for their favorite quilt, participate in a silent auction, and purchase one of the many handmade quilts for sale. New and antique quilts are beautifully displayed on handmade wooden quilt racks.

Even non-quilters in attendance can learn plenty about the craft through fascinating demonstrations. A certified appraiser is on hand to determine quilt values and offer advice on quilt care and repair.

WHEN: Third weekend in September
WHERE: YMCA, Marshal
NEARBY ATTRACTION: Nicholas-Beasley Museum
INFO: www.countrypatchworkquilters.com

86. A Fair Amid Outdoor Art

St. Louis is on the cutting edge of many cultural activities, and the ART FAIR at Laumeier Sculpture Park is unique. The sculpture park is a world-class outdoor art museum, and the fair, which hosts 150 artists and craftsmen from across the county, does not disappoint.

Nationally known, the fair is sponsored in part by the city of Sunset Hills, and there is a nominal admission fee for adults and older children, while kids under five are free.

The 150 exhibitors are juried from more than 1,000 applicants, and among the works for sale are clay pieces, paintings, new media, jewelry, photography, fiber, glass, and wood carvings. Artists happily demonstrate their skills, and a popular children's entertainment area called the Creation Location is available, along with two stages that offer performances.

WHEN: Mother's Day weekend
WHERE: Laumeier Sculpture Park, St. Louis
NEARBY ATTRACTION: Large sculptures throughout the park
INFO: 314-615-5278; www.laumeier.org

Plenty of upscale food vendors are on hand, and visitors should leave time to attend the "Art of the Wine" event, held the night before the fair opens. There they will find wine-tasting offerings from local wineries, adding a touch of class to the event. The twelve-dollar entry fee for the wine event covers unlimited tastings and lovely entertainment by guest musicians.

The park grew from a seventy-two-acre gift from Matilda Laumeier and opened in 1976. The most recent expansion, in 2006, increased its size to 105 acres. A centerpiece of the site is a large, historic, stone-cut home, which is used as a service building.

87. A Peach of an Event

The Missouri Peachfest Growers and the Lexington Chamber of Commerce have created a peachy happening in Lexington. The MISSOURI PEACH FESTIVAL is held each year on the first Saturday in August in downtown Lexington, a haven for fresh produce like perfect peaches.

The day's activities begin with a breakfast of biscuits and gravy at the First United Methodist Church. But from that point on, the festival focuses squarely on its namesake fruit. A downtown bookstore offers peach pies for sale, and contests are held for the best peach cobbler, peach preserve, peach pie, and most savory peach dish.

The festival's best find is a tour of as many as ten local orchards, accessible by hopping on a downtown trolley car for a short ride to see for yourself which growers boast the best tree-ripened peaches.

Lexington is a lovely, historic town located on the Missouri River and the site of the "Battle of Hemp Bales," one of the first clashes of the Civil War. The town's authentic architecture and antebellum homes remain largely intact.

WHEN: First Saturday in August
WHERE: Downtown Lexington
NEARBY ATTRACTIONS: Wineries and antiquing
INFO: 866-837-4711;
660-259-3082;
www.visitlexington.com;
www.historiclexingtonmo.com

Established in 1822, Lexington grew quickly and became one of the most important towns west of St. Louis by 1830. Its name derives from the fact that many of its early settlers were from Kentucky and gave it a name with which they were familiar.

88. A Burst of Sun

Once a year, the historic town of Clarksville decks itself out in brilliant yellows and rich browns for its SUNFLOWER FESTIVAL.

Branded as one of Missouri's best eagle-watching areas, Clarksville departs from that role during the last weekend in July to host an event in which roadsides, fields, alleys, and flowerbeds fill with sunflowers. Visitors can take it all in on foot or by shuttle, with either option offering plenty of great photo opportunities.

The two-day festival takes place in the heat of the summer and attracts artists from nearby states. They come to paint sunflowers or related subjects, while potters pick up on the theme as well by molding pots and accessories. Contestants compete for the coveted People's Choice Award for the best sunflower art created during the festival. Day's end judging takes place at the Apple Shed at 5 p.m.

WHEN: Last weekend of July
WHERE: Streets and fields of Clarksville
NEARBY ATTRACTION: Clarksville Antique Center
INFO: www.clarksvillemo.us

Amid the sunflower theme, a bevy of honey-related foods and activities turn out to be the festival's sweetest find. Beekeepers are on hand to discuss and demonstrate the art and science of their trade. Vendors offer tempting and delicious sunflower seeds in many varieties, and fresh honey and honey-related foods are available as well.

The Clarksville Station, located in the middle of all the activity, offers a photo scene in which visitors can pop their heads through the center of a sunflower to create a sunny remembrance of the weekend.

89. A Field of Bargains

Everyone loves a bargain, and serious bargain hunters love the RUTLEDGE FLEA MARKET, where over the past six decades the little village has hosted an event that gets bigger and better each year.

Rutledge Partners LLC manages acres of farm ground offering spaces for 1,000 dealers, who come from throughout the country and typically occupy more than half of the 25 × 40 foot spaces, which rent for $30 per day or $150 per year.

Flea Market vendors enjoy a culture of their own, with some choosing to camp on the grounds for extended selling periods while other show up only once a year. The variety of bargains includes antique furniture, used goods, farm supplies and equipment, crafts, and animals.

The Flea Market began in 1948 as a gun-and-dog exchange and hillbilly auction. After several moves under multiple owners, it has settled in as one of the most famous markets in the country. The typical vendor might offer guns, clothing, and chickens all in the same booth space. Some of the vendors are local businessmen, like the Mennonite gardener who brings fresh produce from his greenhouse. Half of the population of Rutledge is Mennonite.

Traversing the expansive market on foot can be exhausting, so golf carts are available for rent. Plenty of tasty food is available, including fresh barbeque and funnel cakes.

If you can't find a bargain here, you're unlikely to find it anywhere.

WHEN: March through November, opens at 6:30 a.m.
WHERE: Route V, Rutledge
NEARBY ATTRACTION: Zimmerman's Mennonite Dry Goods Store
INFO: 660-883-5816; www.rutledge-fleamarket.com

90. A Nutty Affair

Missouri's agriculture and culture come together each year in New Franklin at the MISSOURI CHESTNUT ROAST. The fall chestnut harvest season is the centerpiece of a celebration that includes homegrown roasted chestnuts, pecans, and samplings of Missouri's state nut, the black walnut.

Highlights include free tasting samples, educational opportunities, musical entertainment, children's activities, and, of course, chestnut roasts.

More than thirty vendors offer a variety of goods, and the festival provides tours of chestnut orchards and ongoing research areas at the Horticulture and Agroforestry Research Center.

Activity centers on the farm's Thomas Hickman House, which also is the site of the festival's best find. One of Missouri's oldest standing brick homes, the Thomas Hickman House, was built in 1819 and is listed on the National Register of Historic Places.

WHEN: Second Saturday in October
WHERE: University of Missouri Center for Agroforestry's Horticulture and the Agroforestry Research Center, New Franklin
NEARBY ATTRACTION: Thomas Hickman House
INFO: 573-882-3234; www.centerforagroforestry.org

The event is designed to expand the state's offering of nut products, advertise Missouri's nut industry, and attract agri-tourism traffic to the state.

One interesting fact visitors learn at the festival is that the black walnut is the hardest among hardwood trees, and black walnut shells can be used for cleaning metal and employed as dynamite filler.

Meanwhile, the chestnut is the most romantic of nuts, generally associated with roasting over an open fire during the Christmas season.

91. Garden Traditions

Some call Hermann the Sausage Capital of Missouri. Others visit for its many wineries and scenic beauty. The locals, however, love to boast about their beautiful gardens and garden club, which has been meeting for more than seventy-five years.

Flowers and gardens are a central attraction in this historic German community, whose GARDEN TOUR AND PERENNIAL PLANT FESTIVAL has been taking place for thirty years.

The event is sponsored by Hermann's long-established garden club, which, unlike some, is a working club and not an excuse to get together for lunch. Members believe their hands-on approach to gardening is the biggest reason for their success.

At least sixteen unique gardens highlight the festival tour, and an added find is a stop at the home of internationally recognized garden artist Alice Calhoun. Calhoun's charming, historic, brick home greets visitors as they enter the town, and overflowing flowerboxes are a real showstopper.

The artist's lush garden, accessible from the side of the home, is open to visitors free of charge. The English-style garden is a centerpiece for Calhoun's intricate garden ornaments, including metal, fairy-like designs that dot the pathway that runs along the house and garden shed.

The well-attended tour offers plenty of photo opportunities. On the main tour route, guides describe the historic architecture and fountains. Cost for the tour is eight dollars, and tours run from 10 a.m. to 5 p.m.

Some of the garden stops offer delightful refreshments like Lavender tea. The backyard of Strehley Cottage, circa 1830, is home to some of the best Norton grape stock, Missouri's state grape.

WHEN: First weekend in June
WHERE: Historic downtown Hermann
NEARBY ATTRACTION: The German School
INFO: 573-486-5400; 800-932-8687; www.hermannmo.com

92. A Historical Review

The town of Mexico hosts a unique event each year that offers a historical overview of America from colonial times through the Korean War. The LIVING HISTORY FESTIVAL AND COUNTRY FAIR is held each September at Robert S. Green Park, site of Graceland Mansion, built in 1857.

The park provides an ideal backdrop for a walk back through time that includes period actors demonstrating crafts and re-creating the lifestyle of each era.

Sponsored by the Adrian County Historical Society, the event includes eight camps based on different time periods: Native American village, 1770s colonial, 1830s mountain men, 1860s Civil War, 1880s cowboys, 1898 Spanish-American War, 1918 World War I, and finally 1940s World War II. War re-enactments range from the Civil War to World War II.

Other highlights include a vintage baseball tournament and a free tour of restored buildings that includes Firebrick Museum, Prairie View Christian Church, the Country School, and the American Saddle Horse Capital of the World.

Beginning at dusk, visitors are invited to participate in the Saturday Candlelight Tours, which end with campfires.

WHEN: Last weekend in September
WHERE: Robert S. Green Park, Mexico
NEARBY ATTRACTION: Missouri Military Academy
INFO: 800-581-2765

Nostalgic events are always a hit, and folks around the country who are avid fans of historic Route 66 gather in St. Louis each year for the ST. LOUIS ROUTE 66 FESTIVAL.

The ten-hour festival celebrates February 4, 1927, the day U.S. Highway 66 was opened in Missouri, which became the third state to join what would become known variously as the "Main Street of America," "The Mother Road," "The Way West," and "The Will Rogers Highway."

The festival's coolest find is that it occurs on the historic Chain of Rocks Bridge, which closed to all but pedestrian and bicycle traffic in 2006. The bridge has been added to the National Register of Historic Places and remains one of the iconic structures along Route 66.

The festival draws vintage vehicles from as long ago as the 1920s, and at 4 p.m. the Parade of Cars takes place, with a procession of cars coming off the bridge.

Other highlights include musical performances throughout the day and a menu of exceptional "road" food that includes Cozy Dogs (hot dogs on a stick), barbeque, and confections from Ted Drews, the traditional and popular St. Louis frozen custard spot that opened in 1927.

Bobby Troup's 1946 hit song implored listeners to "Get Your Kicks, on Route 66." This festival is the perfect opportunity to heed Troup's advice.

WHEN: First Saturday in October
WHERE: 10950 Riverview Dr. (Chain of Rocks Bridge), St. Louis
NEARBY ATTRACTION: Columbia Bottom Conservation Area
INFO: 314-416-9930; www.confluencegreenway.org

94. A Courthouse Extravaganza

Clinton is home to the largest courthouse in Missouri and one of the largest in the United States, which serves as the site of the OLDE GLORY DAYS FESTIVAL.

The historic town has had its ups and downs. It became the focus of national media attention in 2006, when the Elks Lodge collapsed in downtown Clinton, killing exalted leader Tony Komer just as residents of the town were preparing to celebrate its bicentennial.

Festival activities begin days before the Sunday evening fireworks display. Among the featured events is the Glory Days Lunch on the courthouse lawn. Each year, visitors gather with lawn chairs in tow to take part in a variety of themed lunches ranging from hot dogs to fancy grilled tenderloins. Tickets are limited to the first one thousand diners.

On Sunday morning, local musicians play at the gazebo, and west of the square, a church service is sponsored by the Ministerial alliance. Also that morning, members of the local Knights of Columbus host a biscuits-and-gravy breakfast.

Each day of the festival revolves around the town's sense of patriotism, and a clever find is the outdoor Olde Glory Days Home Decorating Contest. Contestants vie for gift certificates provided by the chamber of commerce. A special award goes to the city block displaying the best community spirit. Participants are encouraged to use banners, bunting, and flags to show off their national pride.

Olde Glory Days is free and welcomes thousands of visitors each year.

WHEN: First weekend in July
WHERE: Courthouse Square, Clinton
NEARBY ATTRACTION: Buildings in the downtown district feature old-fashioned advertising paintings and signs
INFO: 660-885-8166; www.missouridaytrips.com; www.clintonmochamber.com

95. From the Vine to Art

Sedalia has much more to offer than the Missouri State Fair, which is popular in its own right. The city also hosts one of the state's most unique art shows, the SHOW ME GOURD FESTIVAL, which brings in nationally known gourd artists from around the country. Yes, gourds. The familiar fall symbol is a close relative of the pumpkin. Gourds have long tempted the creative soul.

Artist must enter three pieces, and 80 percent of their merchandise must consist of gourds, while the other 20 percent may be crafting materials. Competition is stiff in several categories, with Best Crafter the most coveted award.

Gourds come in all shapes and sizes, and displays showcase oddities like the largest and smallest hard shell, along with gourds with unusual handles, called dippers. Artists employ elaborate techniques, including inlaid work, wood burning, carvings, and intricate hand paintings.

The festival's best find is the featured gourder, a member of the Gourd Society who displays present and past works. The featured gourder creates his own designs and most likely raises his own gourds.

The event also includes a live auction on Saturday afternoon and a festive dinner that evening. Workshops cater to aspiring gourd artists, and imaginations run wild at the Gourd Art Parade.

Missouri has gourd patch gatherings in three geographical regions—St. Louis, Kansas City, and Central Missouri.

WHEN: Last weekend in April
WHERE: State Fairgrounds, Sedalia
NEARBY ATTRACTION: Historic Katy Depot
INFO: 660-826-2222; www.showmegourdsociety1.homestead.com

96. THE RIDES OF SUMMER

Rolla celebrates the beginning of summer with its ROUTE 66 SUMMER-FEST, when hundreds of cars and motorcycles arrive at the St. James Visitor Center on a Friday afternoon and prepare to cruise Route 66 that evening.

The drivers all have the same job—that of transporting queen candidates vying for the title of Miss Route 66. Other Friday events include an evening Poker Run for motorcycle enthusiasts and a skateboarding event for the younger attendees.

Saturday morning's highlights include crafts booths, a Classic Car Show on Pine Street, and a Motorcycle Show on Eighth Street.

The popular Tour-de-Phelps Bicycle Ride to St. James and back kicks off at 8 a.m. The scenic twelve-mile round-trip ride has stops and refreshments along the way. Younger riders—all the way down to tricyclists—gather in front of Meek's Lumberyard for their own mini-tour. Entry fee for the tour is three dollars, with trophies going to the winners. Classes are available for those who want to prepare for next year's races.

WHEN: First weekend in June
WHERE: Downtown Rolla
NEARBY ATTRACTION: Missouri University of Science and Technology
INFO: www.route66summerfest.net

Things kick into high gear on Saturday evening with the event's most dramatic find, when classic cars and motorcycles drive to the festival grounds for the Burn Out Contest. Starting at 5 p.m., spectators gather to see which driver can create the most smoke and produce the most crowd appeal.

97. Port of World Festival

St. Louis has earned its reputation as a diverse city that celebrates people of all nationalities with respect and grandeur. Along those lines, its KWANZAA: FESTIVAL OF THE FIRST FRUITS celebration, started in 1966, is a way for African-Americans and Pan-Africans to promote their culture's unique talents, religion, and beauty.

This event celebrating Kwanzaa, which means "first fruits" in Swahili, is hosted in the Missouri Botanical Garden, which serves as a beautiful location for the seven-day holiday celebration.

At the heart of Kwanzaa are its seven candles—three red on the left and three green on the right centered around a single black candle. The black candle, representing unity, is lit on the first night of Kwanzaa. The red and green candles are then lit, one each day, representing past struggles and future hopes as depicted on a flag created by Marcus Greenway. Each candle stands for one of the seven principals known as Nguzo Saba: unity, self-determination, collective work and responsibility, cooperative economics, purpose, creativity, and faith.

The best find is the opportunity to purchase the exceptional authentic African art, jewelry, and home décor. Another highlight is the entertainment, which includes costumed dancers and musicians performing to the beat of African drums. Ethnic food vendors abound, offering a savory selection of dishes.

A large number of Kwanzaa's supporters are African-American professionals who seek to promote and protect a sense of African-American pride for future generations. Admission to the garden includes the Kwanzaa celebration, which otherwise is free.

WHEN: Last weekend in December
WHERE: Missouri Botanical Garden, St. Louis
NEARBY ATTRACTION: Missouri Botanical Garden's other attractions
INFO: 314-577-9400; www.mobot.org

98. PADDLE TO VICTORY

Do you enjoy the challenge and beauty of the Missouri River? Then you might want to consider entering your canoe or kayak in the annual MISSOURI RIVER 340 RACE.

The well-known race begins in Kansas City and ends in St. Charles at the Lewis and Clark Boathouse and Nature Center. Dubbed the world's longest, non-stop river race, it is a grueling event that requires boaters to reach eight checkpoints along the river in fewer than eighty-eight hours. The checkpoints are located in Lexington, Waverley, Miami, Glasgow, Cooper's Landing, Jefferson City, Hermann, and Washington. Failure to meet two consecutive checkpoint deadlines is grounds for disqualification. Generally, about two-thirds of those who start the race end up completing the course.

The scenery is beautiful, but the race is physically demanding, including a variety of rapids, locks, and portages that must be traversed. Sandbars, bridge pilings, and other boaters and barges represent further challenges, and, not surprisingly, boating through the night is tiring. Other challenges include mosquitoes, heat, fog, and storms—enough to test even the most experienced boater.

The river towns along the route enthusiastically greet participants, offering meals and conveniences. Paddlers may stop whenever they want to, but assistance is prohibited and no rowing, sailing, or other propulsion is permitted.

The winning team receives trophies, cash prizes, and medals.

WHEN: Late July each year
WHERE: Kaw Kaw Point, Kansas City
NEARBY ATTRACTIONS: Historic towns along the way
INFO: 913-244-4666; www.confluencegreenway.org; www.rivermiles.com

99. SIGHTS AND SOUNDS OF HALLOWEEN

For more than sixty years, the Independence Chamber of Commerce has been thrilling residents with a festival of goblins, ghosts, and witches at its annual HALLOWEEN PARADE. With the help of Centerpoint Medical Center, organizers create a spectacular Halloween experience.

This is no ordinary street parade—it's the city's longest parade, and it incorporates school groups, businesses, car clubs, dance studios, and individual marchers. Led by the colorful William Chresman High School Marching Bruins, participants try to outdo each other with costumes in categories ranging from storybook characters to the scariest witch.

WHEN: October 31 at 3 p.m.
WHERE: Historic Independence Square, Independence
NEARBY ATTRACTION: Harry Truman Library and Museum
INFO: 816-252-4745; www.independencechamber.org

Floats must follow a Halloween theme and are judged in four main categories, with trophies awarded to the first- and second-place entries in each category.

Designated merchants on the town square offer trick-or-treating from 1 p.m. to 3 p.m. before the parade begins. A magnificent monster pumpkin at the Community American Credit Union challenges visitors to guess its weight.

One of the popular and scary finds are the parade's sounds, particularly the Ghost Riders, who are costumed motorcycle riders who gun their engines. More nostalgic are the antique cars driven by Halloween characters.

The parade is held rain or shine.

100. STRIKE UP THE BANDS

WHEN: Third weekend in October
WHERE: NCM Fairgrounds, Trenton
NEARBY ATTRACTION: North Central Missouri State College
INFO: 660-359-4324; www.trentonmochamber.com

Trenton, population six thousand, is a special Missouri community in many ways. In 1915, the Missouri General Assembly designated Missouri Day as the third Wednesday in October. Governor Arthur M. Hyde, a Trenton native, fittingly made the proclamation.

Hyde's hometown celebrates its heritage each year with the MISSOURI DAY FESTIVAL, which has grown and prospered since it began twenty-five years ago.

More than two hundred vendors now attend what has become a sellout event, nestled inside and outside the North Central Missouri Fairgrounds and 1940s era octagon-shaped stone barn. Trenton's Friends of the Library gather used books to sell, utilizing space inside the barn, which is used year-round for other town events.

Highlights include a baby show, town hall dance, flea market booths, crafters, and antique booths. Be sure to save some loose change for the festival food, which features favorites like sweet potato fries, blooming fried onions, fried tenderloins, and fried ribbon potato fries.

The best find at this fun-filled festival is the gathering of marching bands that come to Trenton to compete against one another. More than fifty bands arrive in busloads from nearby states to tout their musical talent and marching skills. They provide entertainment throughout the festival, and when the students aren't performing they become festival-goers.

Missouri pride is at its best during the event, with volunteers working hard to make sure everyone has a good time. Missouri is the Show Me State, and Trenton lives up to that mission during the Missouri Festival.

SOURCES

In addition to personal interviews, the following people, websites, and publications assisted me in obtaining information about the featured festivals.

1. www.truefalse.org; www.visitcolumbiamo. com; Cooper, *The Missouri Quick Fact Book*, MRI; *Missouri Life Magazine*, Feb. 2000.

2. www.stcharleschristmas.com; www.historicstcharles.com; St. Charles Visitors and Convention Bureau; *Missouri Life Magazine*, June 2009.

3. www.lindenwood.edu/boone; www.slfp. com/ETC-PioneerDays; Betty and Bob Moore; St. Charles Convention and Visitors Bureau.

4. www.colemanhawkins.org; www.st.jo.com; Godley and O'Rourke, *Daytrip Missouri*.

5. www.saxon/lutheranmemorial.com; www.visitmo.com; www.eastperrylumber. com; Hazelwood, *100 Unique Eats and Eateries of Missouri*.

6. www.hartsburgpumpkinfest.com; Cooper, *The Missouri Quick Fact Book*, MRI; Hazelwood, *100 Best Kept Secrets of Missouri*; *A to Z Dictionary of Missouri*, Pebble Publishing.

7. www.chilicookoff.com.

8. www.charlestonmo.org; Hazelwood, *100 Best Kept Secrets of Missouri*; *Missouri Life Magazine*, April 2009.

9. www.waltdisneymuseum.org/about; *Missouri Life Magazine*, Aug. 2008.

10. www.chillicothenews.com; www. homeofslicedbread.com; Hazelwood, *100 Best Kept Secrets of Missouri*; *Missouri Life Magazine*, April 2009.

11. www.eastprariemo.net; *Missouri Life Magazine*, June 2008; Slivey Barber.

12. www.branson-missouri.com; Olson, *Rural Missouri Magazine*, 2008; Cooper, *The Missouri Quick Fact Book*, MRI.

13. www.elmsresort.com; chamber of commerce, Elms Hotel brochure and flyer.

14. www.goboonville.com; www.bigmuddy. org; www.friendsofhistoricboonville.org;

Hazelwood, *100 Best Kept Secrets of Missouri*; Boonville Visitors Guide.

15. www.visitmo.com; www.calmo.com; *Missouri Life Magazine*, 2008; *A to Z Dictionary of Missouri*, Pebble Publishing.

16. James Ellis; www.salemmo.com.

17. www.richmondchamber.com; Delano and Gicento, *Off the Beaten Path*; Hazelwood, *100 Best Kept Secrets of Missouri*.

18. www.ci.sedalia.mo.us; www.scottjoplin. org; Godley and O'Rourke, *Daytrip Missouri*; Kogut, *Show Me Romance*.

19. Carrollton Chamber of Commerce; Linda Levo of Norborne; Hazelwood, *100 Best Kept Secrets of Missouri*.

20. www.missouriliteraryfestival.org; www. macca.net.

21. www.visithannibal.com; www.hannibaljaycees.org; Satterfield, *Backroads & Byways of Missouri*; Holly Henderson of Hannibal; *Missouri Life*, June 2009; Kenny Hulshop State Rep., 9th District.

22. www.kcirishfest.com; *Missouri Life Magazine*, Aug. 2008.

23. www.historicstcharles.com; www. lewisandclarkheritagedays.com.

24. www.woodennickelrestaurant.com/r66; Dan Vogt.

25. www.stlouisgreekfest.com; St. Louis Calendar of Events; *St. Louis Post-Dispatch*, Sept. 7, 2009.

26. www.appleblossomparade.com/abhistory; Ken Rosenwasser, St. Joseph; *Missouri Life Magazine*, April 2007 and Feb. 2008.

27. www.greatriverroad.com; Cooper, *The Missouri Quick Fact Book*, MRI; Richard Gebhardt and Shawn Long, Ste. Genevieve.

28. www.springfield-missouri.blogspot.com; Amy Duley, Park Coordinator; *Missouri Life Magazine*, June 2009.

29. www.emissourian.com; Hazelwood, *100 Best Kept Secrets of Missouri*; Barb Hannon, state tourism office.

30. www.kcchalkandwalk.org; *Missouri Life Magazine*, June 2009.

31. www.sdcculinarycraftschool.com/classes; www.silverdollarcity.com; Barb Hannon, state tourism office.

32. www.worldsheepfest.com; Donna Parsons, chairman of festival.

33. www.explorstlouis.com; Jasper Notto, St. Charles; Hazelwood, *100 Unique Eats and Eateries of Missouri*; *Missouri Life Magazine*, 2006; Hazelwood, *100 Best Kept Secrets of Missouri*.

34. www.funlake.com; www.versailleschamber.com; Cooper, *The Missouri Quick Fact Book*, MRI; Barb Hannon, state tourism office.

35. www.historicstcharles.com; www.examiner.com; Rose Thro, St. Charles.

36. www.waynesvilledailyguide.com; www.pulaskicountydaily.com, article by Darrell Todd Maurina.

37. www.ozarkmountainmuledays.com; www.donkeys.com/info; *Missouri Life Magazine*, Aug. 2008.

38. www.visitmo.com/listing; www.lstourism.com; Gary Sutton, Lee Summit; Hazelwood, *100 Best Kept Secrets of Missouri*; *Kansas City Star*, Kevin Collison.

39. www.mobot.org; Hazelwood, *100 Best Kept Secrets of Missouri*; Barb Hannon, state tourism office.

40. www.cherryblossomfest.com; www.marshfieldmochamberofcommerce.com; *A to Z Dictionary of Missouri*, Pebble Publishing.

41. www.arrowrock.org; *Missouri Life Magazine*, April 2009.

42. www.brumleymusic.com; www.lebanmissouri.org; *Missouri Life Magazine*, Aug. 2008; Cooper, *The Missouri Quick Fact Book*, MRI.

43. www.kcshakes.org.

44. www.hispanicfestival.com; www.stlbeacon.org/region; Nancy Hillberg, chairman; committee member Bud Millheiser.

45. www.walterbargen.com; www.kmos.org;

Ryan King, night manager of vineyard; *Missouri Life Magazine*, April 2009.

46. www.joplinglobe.com; www.boomtowndays.com; Jeff Meredith and Ginger Lamar, Joplin Chamber of Commerce.

47. www.associatedcontent.com; www.iistl.org/festival.php; www.tps.cr.nps.gov/nhl/detail.

48. www.vacationsmadeeasy.com; www.springfieldmo.gov; www.answers.com; *Missouri Life*, Aug. 2008.

49. www.mostatefair.com; www.mostatefairfoundation.net; *Missouri Life*, Aug. 2008.

50. www.colecamp.com; Margie Maxwell; *Missouri Life Magazine*, Aug. 2009; Hazelwood, *100 Best Kept Secrets of Missouri*.

51. www.nixa.k12.mo/districtinfo/suckerdays; www.50states.com/facts; Godley and O'Rourke, *Daytrip Missouri*.

52. www.oldtimemusic.org.

53. www.eventlister.com/E1192780; www.culturemob.com/events; www.bransonshows.com; *Missouri Life Magazine*, Aug. 2009.

54. www.persimmonhill.com; www.news.branson.com, June 5, 2009; *Missouri Life*, Aug. 2006.

55. www.downtownpoplarbluff.com.

56. www.stlcls.org; www.tripcart.com.

57. www.warrenton-mo.org; Jan Olearnick, chamber of commerce.

58. www.jamesportmo.org; www.amishretail.com; Jamesport travel booklet.

59. www.perryvillemo.com; www.nca-usa.org/psp/perryville; *Missouri Life*, 2006.

60. www.powellgardens.org; Roland Tehibault of Lee Summit; *Rural Missouri Magazine*, 2006.

61. www.kcscottishgames.org; *Missouri Life Magazine*, June 2008.

62. www.walnutspringsfarm.com; www.fghps.org; Kathy Brown, owner of farm; *Missouri Life Magazine*, April 2005.

63. www.events.stltoday.com; www.polishfalcons.org; Folkfire Folk Dance & Music Calendar; Royce Schierding, St. Charles.

64. www.winecountrygarden.net; Chris Shaul, Defiance; Hazelwood, *100 Best Kept Secrets of Missouri.*

65. www.mcwra.net; McEowen, *Missouri Rural Magazine*, Sept. 2009; Gene Gann.

66. www.caruthersvillecity.com; Christina Weber, chamber of commerce.

67. www.stjoesnews.net; www.parisheson-line.com; *Missouri Life Magazine*, June 2009.

68. www.neoshomo.org; Hazelwood, *100 Best Kept Secrets of Missouri.*

69. www.festivalofthelittlehills.com; Bob Scott, St. Charles.

70. www.rizstakesandfunnelcakes.com; www.c-magic.com/salisbury/events; Wikipedia's explanation of Salisbury steak.

71. www.bearcatgetaway.com; www.festivalnet.com.

72. www.arcadiavalley.biz/civilwar; www.missourihistorictowns.com.

73. www.farmcollector.com; www.westonmo.com; Weston brochure; Bonnie Stewart, chamber of commerce.

74. www.festivalnet.com; www.eviesays.com/event.

75. www.missouriwaterfowlfestival.com; www.kennettmo.com.

76. www.missourimansion.org; *Missouri Life*, 2005.

77. www.mountainviewmo.com; www.mountainview.macaa.net.

78. www.lasr.net/travel/city; www.wikapedia.org; Hazelwood, *100 Best Kept Secrets of Missouri*; Judi Baldwin, picnic secretary.

79. www.kdbsites.com/chamber; Sarah Hahensee, chamber of commerce.

80. www.blackwater-mo.com; Bonnie Rapp and Gerald Cunningham, Blackwater.

81. www.fayettenewspapers.com/content; Connie Shay, Fayette.

82. www.slfp.com/ETC-BalloonRace; www.greatforestparkbaloonrace.com; Keaggy, *St. Louis Post-Dispatch.*

83. www.visitsikeston-miner.com; www.standard-democrat.com/story; www.dddnews.com/story; Sikeston and Miner brochure.

84. www.tower-rock-winery.com; www.rosecity.net/rhr/perry; Imogene Unger and Pearlene Deganhardt, Frohna.

85. www.countrypatchworkquilters.com; Betty Lenz, Michael Marsh, and Karen Gutherie, Marshal; quilt show brochure.

86. www.laumeiersculpturepark.org; Hazelwood, *100 Best Kept Secrets of Missouri*; Barb Hannon, state tourism office.

87. www.visitlexington.com; www.visitmo.com; www.historiclexington.com; *Missouri Life Magazine*, Aug. 2009.

88. www.saucemagazine.com; www.clarksvillemo.us; Marini Ross, O'Fallon; *Missouri Life Magazine*, July 2009.

89. www.rutledge-fleamarket.com; www.missouritourism.org; *Missouri Life Magazine*, 2003, Bob Sands, Unionville.

90. www.centerforagroforestry.org; Carole Marsh, *My First Pocket Guide to Missouri.*

91. www.hermann.com; Hermann fall 2009 visitors guide; Pat and Jack Wendleton, Hermann.

92. www.audrain.org; *Missouri Life Magazine*, Aug. 2009, Mexico Chamber of Commerce.

93. www.confluencegreenway.org; www.missouri66.org; Kathy Weilbacher, manager; Chuck Morley, O'Fallon.

94. www.missouridaytrips.com; www.clintonmochamber.com; Megan Asbill, director.

95. www.showmegourdssociety1.homestead.com; www.ciosedalia.mo.us.

96. www.route66summerfest.net; Godley and O'Rourke, *Daytrip Missouri.*

97. www.soulofamerica.com; www.findarticles.com; www.associatedcontent.com.

98. www.rivermiles.com; *Rural Missouri Magazine*, Sept. 2007; Kathy Weilbacher, P.R. director, Mimi Jackson, St. Charles.

99. www.independencechamber.org.

100. www.trentonmochamber.com; Kathy Thrasher, Trenton.

LOCATIONS BY REGION

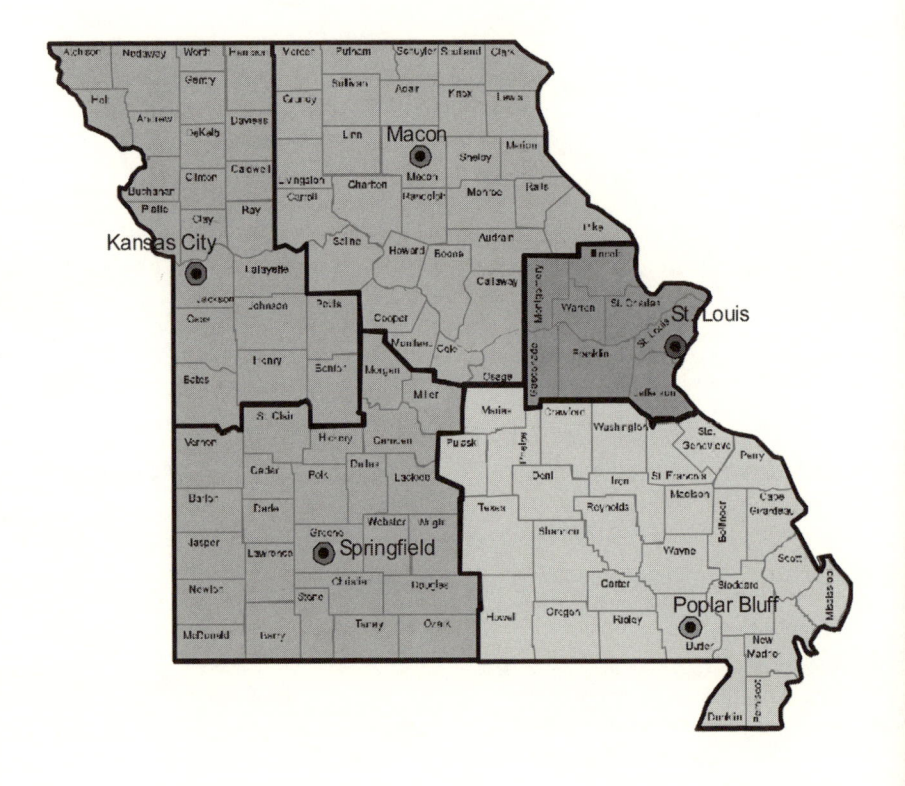

Kansas City

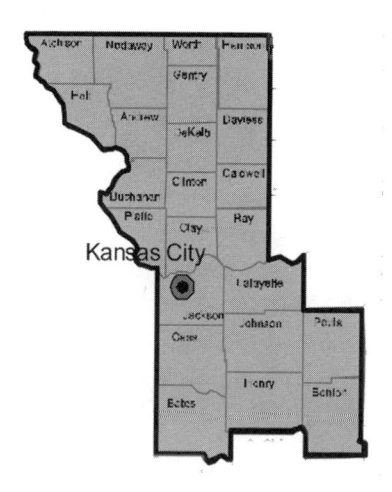

4. St. Joseph, Coleman Hawkins Legacy Jazz Festival

13. Excelsior Springs, Waterfest

17. Richmond, Mushroom Festival

18. Sedalia, Scott Joplin Ragtime Festival

19. Norborne, Soybean Festival

22. Kansas City, Irish Fest

26. St. Joseph, Apple Blossom Parade

30. Kansas City, Chalk & Walk Festival

38. Lee Summit, Fall Festival

43. Kansas City, Heart of America Shakespeare Festival

49. Sedalia, Missouri State Fair

58. Jamesport, Amish Quilt Auction

60. Kingsville, Festival of Butterflies

61. Riverside, Scottish Highland Games

67. St. Joseph, St. Patrick's Mexican Fiesta

73. Weston, Lions Club Antique and Collectibles Show

87. Lexington, Missouri Peach Festival

94. Clinton, Olde Glory Days Festival

98. Kansas City, Missouri River 340 Race

99. Independence, Halloween Parade

SPRINGFIELD

12. Branson, Christmas in Branson

20. Springfield, Missouri Literary Festival

28. Springfield, Dairy Days

31. Branson, World-Fest

37. Springfield, Ozark Mountain Mule and Donkey Days

40. Marshfield, Cherry Blossom Festival

42. Lebanon, Brumley Gospel Sing

46. Joplin, Boomtown Days

48. Springfield, Japanese Fall Festival

51. Nixa, Sucker Days

53. Hollister, Grape and Fall Festival

54. Lampe, Persimmon Hill Blueberry Festival and Music Fest

62. Fair Grove, Fair Grove Heritage Reunion

68. Neosho, Annual Dogwood Tour

74. Mt. Vernon, Not So Square Arts Festival

78. El Dorado Springs, Founders Day Picnic

79. Monett, Festival of Lights

95. Sedalia, Show Me Gourd Festival

MACON

1. Columbia, True/False Film Fest

6. Hartsburg, Pumpkin Festival

9. Marceline, Toonfest

10. Chillicothe, Breadfest

14. Boonville, Big Muddy Folk Festival

15. California, Ozark Ham and Turkey Festival

21. Hannibal, Tom Sawyer Days

24. Kirksville, Round Barn Blues Show

32. Ethel, World Sheep & Fiber Festival

34. Versailles, Olde Tyme Apple Festival

36. Waynesville, Frog Fest

41. Arrow Rock, Spring Garden Show and Taste of Missouri

45. Montserrat, Montserrat Poetry Festival

50. Cole Camp, Jim Maxwell Antique Bicycle Show

70. Salisbury, Salisbury Steak Festival

76. Jefferson City, Holiday Candlelight Tour

80. Blackwater, Native American Living Culture Event

81. Fayette, Boonslick Folk Festival

85. Marshall, Country Patchwork Quilt Guild Show

88. Clarksville, Sunflower Festival

89. Rutledge, Flea Market

90. New Franklin, Missouri Chestnut Roast

91. Hermann, Garden Tour and Perennial Plant Festival

92. Mexico, Living History Festival and Country Fair

100. Trenton, Missouri Day Festival

ST. LOUIS

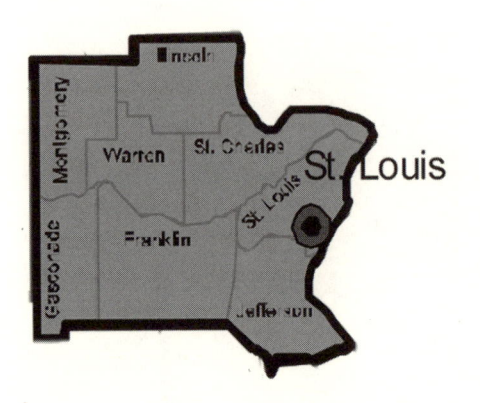

POPLAR BLUFF

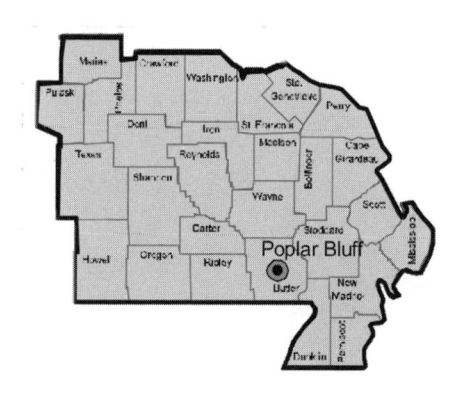

8. Charleston, Dogwood-Azalea Festival

11. East Prairie, Sweetcorn Festival

16. Salem, Upper Current River Pow Wow

27. Ste. Genevieve, French Heritage Festival

29. Washington, Fine Art Fair and Winefest

52. West Plains, Old Time Music Ozark Heritage Festival

55. Poplar Bluff, Oz Festival

59. Perryville, St. Vincent de Paul Seminary Picnic

65. Raymondville, Chuckwagon Racing

66. Caruthersville, White Glove Gala

71. Lesterville, Parrot Head Beach Party

72. Pilot Knob, Battle of Pilot Knob Re-enactment

75. Kennett, Missouri Waterfowl Festival

77. Mt. View, Missouri Cowboy Poetry Festival

83. Sikeston, Cotton Carnival

84. Altenburg, East Perry Fair

96. Rolla, Route 66 Summerfest

Photo Credits

Unless noted, all images were provided by the local chambers of commerce or the festival and event planners. Specific photographers are listed below.

Page 2: courtesy Karen Godfrey

Page 8: courtesy Melissa D. Graham

Page 11: courtesy Barb Hannon

Page 23: courtesy Karen Godfrey

Page 29: courtesy Curt Dennison

Page 34: courtesy Scott Gladden/Lake of the Ozarks Convention & Visitor Bureau, FunLake.com

Page 39: courtesy Missouri Botanical Garden; photo by Erin Whitson

Page 43: courtesy Jan Rogge as Gertrude and Mark Robbins as Claudius in the Heart of America Shakespeare Festival's 2003 production of *Hamlet*; photo by Doug Hamer

Page 47: courtesy International Institute

Page 49: courtesy Missouri State Fair

Page 50: courtesy *Cole Camp Courier*, Cole Camp, MO

Page 56: courtesy Missouri Botanical Garden; photo by Brent Johnston

Page 60: courtesy morguefile

Page 68: courtesy the *Neosho Daily News*

Page 76: courtesy Missouri Governor's Office

Page 86: courtesy Mike Venso/Laumeier Sculpture Park.

Page 90: courtesy University of Missouri Center for Agroforestry

Page 95: courtesy Bert Petrie

Page 97: courtesy Missouri Botanical Garden; photo by Leslie Wallace

Page 99: courtesy Kelo Berkstresser

cover images are from the following festivals, from top left to bottom right: Sunflower Festival, Dogwood Azalea Festival, Kwanzaa (MOBOT, Josh Monken), Show Me Gourd Festival, Heart of America Shakespeare Festival (Doug Hamer), Garden Tour and Perennial Plant Festival (Melissa D. Graham), Pioneer Days, Missouri Chestnut Roast, Missouri Peach Festival.

About the Author

Ann Hazelwood is a Missouri native, born in Perryville. Her adult life brought her to Historic St. Charles, where she restored a historic home and raised her two sons, Joel and Jason.

In 1979, she opened Patches etc. on the street where she lived. As her career developed, she became a Certified Quilt Appraiser, which takes her around the country for lectures and services. She is also a recognized quilt book author for the American Quilting Society and president of the National Quilt Museum, both located in Paducah, Kentucky.

In 2009, Ann sold her business to another owner to be able to spend more time writing. *100 Festive Finds in Missouri* is her fourth book on Missouri. Her previous Show Me State titles include *100 Things To Do In and Around St. Charles*, *100 Best Kept Secrets of Missouri*, and *100 Unique Eats and Eateries in Missouri*.

Ann's love of her home state has inspired her to lecture on *Missouri Travel*. She feels Missouri has offered her a wonderful quality of life, and she wants to share it with you.